Joseph Fessler

The True and the False Infallibility of the Popes

A Controversial Reply to Dr. Schulte

Joseph Fessler

The True and the False Infallibility of the Popes
A Controversial Reply to Dr. Schulte

ISBN/EAN: 9783337032821

Printed in Europe, USA, Canada, Australia, Japan

Cover: Foto ©ninafisch / pixelio.de

More available books at **www.hansebooks.com**

THE TRUE AND THE FALSE

INFALLIBILITY OF THE POPES.

A Controversial Reply to Dr. Schulte.

BY

Dr. JOSEPH FESSLER,
LATE BISHOP OF ST. POLTEN, IN AUSTRIA,
AND SECRETARY-GENERAL OF THE VATICAN COUNCIL.

A Work honoured by a Brief of Approbation from His Holiness Pope Pius IX.

Translated from the Third Edition
BY PERMISSION OF THE EDITORS OF THE LATE BISHOP FESSLER'S WORKS.

LONDON: BURNS AND OATES,
Portman Street and Paternoster Row.
1875.

Extract from a Brief addressed to Bishop Fessler by his Holiness Pope Pius IX.

April 27, 1871.

'.... PEROPPORTUNUM autem et utilissimum existimavimus retudisse te audaciam Professoris Schulte incitantis sæculares Potestates adversus dogma Pontificiæ infallibilitatis ab œcumenicâ Vaticanâ Synodo definitæ. Non omnes enim, inter laicos præsertim, rei indolem perspectam habent; et veritas luculenter exposita multas abigere solet ab honestorum mentibus obliquas opiniones, sæpe cum lacte haustas, aliosque confirmare in rectâ sententiâ et adversus insidias munire. Quamobrem si hujusmodi commenta refellere pergas, optime certe merebis de sanctissimâ religione nostrâ et Christiano populo, quem, uti bonus Pastor, a venenatis pascuis abduces. Pergratum Nos tibi profitemur animum, cum ob volumen oblatum, tum ob amantissimas litteras tuas; tibique amplam apprecamur obsequii devotionisque tuæ mercedem.....'

Translation.

'...WE esteem it a very opportune and useful thing to have beaten back the audacity of Professor Schulte, inciting as he does the secular powers against the dogma of Papal Infallibility, as defined by the Ecumenical Council of the Vatican. For it is a matter the true meaning of which, not all men, and especially not all laymen, have a thoroughly clear understanding of, and the truth, when lucidly set forth, is wont to expel from properly constituted minds opinions which men perhaps have drunk in with their mother's milk, to confirm others in a right mind, and fortify them against insidious attacks. Wherefore, if you continue to refute figments of this kind, you will deserve well of our most holy religion, and of all Christian people, in that, like a good pastor, you withdraw them from poisoned pastures. We make known to you, then, the great pleasure you have given Us, both by reason of the book which you have presented to Us, as well as by reason of your most affectionate letters; and We pray that you may receive a rich reward for your deference to Our authority and devotion towards Ourselves. . . . .'

(*Signed by the Pope's own hand.*)

NOTE.—The fact of the Brief and its signature is derived from M. Anton. Erdinger, director of the Episcopal Seminary at St. Polten, author of the Life of Bishop Fessler, who sent a copy of it to M. Cosquin of the *Français*, to whom I am indebted for these important notices. The Pope's Brief is not given entire, as the remainder of it has reference solely to local diocesan affairs.

TRANSLATOR'S INTRODUCTION.

THIS important work of the lamented Dr. Fessler, Bishop of St. Polten, or more properly St. Hippolytus, in Austria, who was Secretary-General to the Vatican Council in the year 1870, and who, worn out with the fatigues of the Council, died two years afterwards, is now for the first time brought before the notice of English Catholics.

Entitled by the good Bishop himself *The True and False Infallibility of the Pope*, it presents to the reader a perfect 'repertorium' of all the stock objections and erroneous representations, both as regards the doctrine itself, and as regards the history of previous Papal rescripts and acts, that the fertile mind and extensive reading of Dr. Schulte, Professor of Canon and German Law in the University of Prague, could ingeniously pile together and misconstrue, in order to bring odium upon all Papal Bulls and Papal acts from, as he says, the time of Pope Gregory VII.

These misstatements and misconstructions Bishop Fessler, with extraordinary labour and patience, has met and refuted one by one. The refutations remained unanswered during the Bishop's lifetime, nor have we heard of Dr. Schulte having attempted any answer since his death, although he has gone on reiterating his former statements. It is the old story of 'mumpsimus.' Nevertheless, as this particular mumpsimus is of German extraction, it has been thought that it would not be amiss, while German meets German in this strife of the True and of the False Infallibility, they should carry on the battle in English, that we, who have an equal interest in the issue of the contest, may hear both sides, and judge for ourselves which is the *true* and which the *false*.

And it is this which constitutes the special merit of Bishop Fessler's work, that, in this properly German quarrel, it states fairly all that Dr. Schulte has to say on his own side, so that although we have not actually his book before us, we can hear him speak both in the titles of the chapters and in the propositions brought forward, all of which are given in Dr. Schulte's own words; thus the reader, be he Catholic or be he Protestant, may see for himself what has been said on the part of those who have tried to make Infallibility impossible, by the process of *reductio ad absurdum*, and what by those who calmly and dispassionately have endeavoured to bring it back to its true significance.

It is strange that considering the general interest of the subject, the comprehensive character of the work, its general acceptation in Germany, and, lastly, the author's thorough knowledge of his subject, which his peculiar position during the Council, as its Secretary-General, enabled him to obtain, that so valuable a work should have remained so long untranslated. And this becomes the more remarkable when we consider that after the first edition had been sent to Rome, and there thoroughly examined and approved, the second and third editions were published after the Pope himself had written to Bishop Fessler commending him for having, by means of this work, 'as a good pastor done good service to our holy religion,' and exhorting him to go on 'bringing back Christian people from poisoned pastures;' the particular 'poisoned pastures' indicated by the Pope being evidently those false and exaggerated notions of Infallibility which Dr. Schulte and others of his stamp have been engaged in propagating.

It will be a further good result of the present controversy if it brings us to see the danger of all exaggerated statements, even when made with good intentions, for it is precisely to these statements that the now open adversaries of the Church appeal, in order to place the true doctrine before their dupes in an odious form. And this good result has already followed from the French translation, edited by M. Emmanuel Cosquin, editor of the *Français*. It has 'put the question before many, who had been made anxious by exaggerated statements, in a way which rendered it quite easy of acceptance.' The existence of this translation was, I regret to say, not known to me until my own translation from the original was completed; in fact the editor kindly sent me a copy when he saw my advertisement of the pamphlet in the newspapers, accompanied with the obliging permission to make use of his prefatory matter, his valuable notes from the 'Pastoral Instruction' of the Swiss Bishops, and the useful and comprehensive index at the end of his edition. As a most valuable confirmation of the position assumed by Bishop Fessler, I would refer my readers to M. Cosquin's two notes, which I have translated from the French, and appended to the second chapter of this work.

That Bishop Fessler was really the exponent of the mind of most of the German Bishops, and in particular that his work exercised a special influence on the learned historian of the Councils, Mgr. Hefele, Bishop of Rothenburg, will be sufficiently shown by the following letter, translated from the *Germania*, the organ of the Catholics of Berlin, whose editor, Herr Majunke, although a deputy in the German Assembly, is now undergoing his sentence, as a confessor for the Faith, in a common German prison.

Extract from the Roman correspondent of the *Germania* of Berlin, of Nov. 3, 1872:

'Rome, Oct. 26.

'The letter of Bishop Hefele, which has lately been published, gave rise to an explanation on the part of this prelate; as a result of which the following information came to my knowledge, which, on account of its high importance, I think I ought not to withhold from your readers, and so much the more as it concerns our lately deceased and universally honoured Bishop of St. Polten. Mgr. Fessler, who was on very intimate terms with Dr. Hefele, the Bishop of Rothenburg, sent to him, accompanied with a most affectionate letter, expressive of all those feelings which he entertained towards him as a brother in the episcopal office, a copy of the work which he had composed *On the True and False Infallibility of the Popes*, then just published by Sartori of Vienna. At the same time he had forwarded his pamphlet to all

Introduction.

the other Bishops, no matter what opinion they might have held before the 18th of July 1870. From most of the Bishops Mgr. Fessler received the most sincere congratulations in respect of the work which he had just composed. The Bishop of St. Polten had also previously forwarded it to Pius IX. The Pope had thereupon directed a translation of it to be made into Italian, and instructed a commission of learned theologians of different nationalities to examine it, and report upon it. Both of these commands were put into execution without delay. The Pope made himself thoroughly acquainted with the contents of Bishop Fessler's work, and as his own judgment of it fully corresponded with the judgment of the commission, he wrote a letter with his own hand to the Bishop of St. Polten, praising him for this highly valuable work, and begging him to persevere in the laborious task he had undertaken of correcting the erroneous opinions which had been spread abroad in various directions. Upon the receipt of this Brief Bishop Fessler published a second and third edition of his pamphlet. The Bishop of Rothenburg, however, had declared that although after a thorough examination he perfectly agreed in principle with Fessler's defence of the Vatican definition against Dr. Schulte's pamphlet, still he doubted if the views there maintained would be accepted as sound at Rome. Hereupon the Bishop of St. Polten told him what had happened at Rome about his work, and mentioned that he had received from the Pope himself a letter avowing his satisfaction with it; he also gave Mgr. Hefele this further consoling assurance, that both he himself and many other bishops who gave their *votum* in favour of Infallibility had held this view of the Infallibility of the Pope. The deceased prelate was, however, too simple and too modest to allow this Brief of the Holy Father to be printed in the preface to the second edition of his work.'

The same journal, the *Germania*, adds the following editorial comment on the above: 'The Pastoral Letter of the Bishop of Rothenburg of April 10, 1871, in which he published the Vatican Decree, testifies to the correctness of our Roman correspondent, by the frequent quotations it makes of Bishop Fessler's work *On the True and False Infallibility.*'*

It has been the apparently inevitable result of all Councils that whilst they have settled and confirmed the faith of many, they have left some still anxious as to the exact meaning of the definitions of the fathers there assembled, viz. whether they were to be interpreted with this or that limitation; the question with such persons being, not whether God had spoken by the Council, but whether in what the Council had said, He had meant this or that. The Vatican Council has been no exception to this rule. But how soon and how readily difficulties have been made up since the definition of the Infallibility of the Pope in his teaching office! The chief country of these difficulties was Germany, and what has been the spectacle

* NOTE. As Bishop Hefele published his Pastoral in April 10, 1871, and the Pope's Brief to Mgr. Fessler is dated April 27 of the same year, it is evident that Bishop Hefele had become satisfied that Bishop Fessler's pamphlet expressed the true sentiments of the Holy See on the subject of Infallibility *before* the Pope's Brief reached its author.

presented to our view since the definition of Infallibility, and the publication of Bishop Fessler's pamphlet upon its true meaning? Those Bishops who doubted the opportuneness of the definition, or who in other ways hesitated to receive it, and who, for conscience' sake, absented themselves from the final and decisive session,* have since become the chief confessors and witnesses of the doctrine, before a cruel and persecuting government! Nor has any word of reproach against the Council or the Holy See escaped them in their many trials. Never has an Episcopate been more unanimous, or more patiently endured persecution for the faith. On the other side, viz. of those who have denied the authority of the living Church, speaking in her last and most numerous assembly, what is the spectacle which is presented to us by Dr. Schulte and his friends at the present moment? Not content with assailing the Vatican Council and Pope Pius IX., they assail all Councils, all sayings and doings of Popes since the first eight centuries, differing therein in nothing but name from other Protestant and heretical sects, whose principle is really identical with their own. Both the one and the other have their reward: the one, the Archbishop of Cologne, is earning a martyr's crown in the common gaol, condemned like a felon to forced labour;† the other, Dr. Schulte, has been rewarded with a professorship at the University of Bonn!

* See the account given by Bishop Fessler of their conduct, in the first chapter of his work.
† See *Tablet* newspaper,' Dec. 26. Paul Melchers (the Archbishop) entered on the prison books as 'strawplaiter.'

Here I will conclude this Introduction with a short notice of this gentleman, Bishop Fessler's opponent, Dr. Schulte, whose name has so much prominence in the following pages; it is taken from M. Cosquin's introduction to the French translation.

'Dr. Schulte is a Westphalian by birth, up to the present time (1873) Professor of Canon and German Law at the University of Prague, and a short time since appointed by the Prussian Government to a chair at the University of Bonn. For a long time he enjoyed a well-earned reputation as a canonist, not only by reason of his erudition and the originality which distinguished his works, but also by his strict orthodoxy. The only reproach brought against his writings was their incompleteness, and the obscure form into which they were thrown. About the year 1862, tendencies to unsound doctrines manifested themselves in him, and from the year 1868 these tendencies became more and more pronounced. In 1869 his hand was thought to be seen in the odious compilation, the *Pope and the Council*, published under the assumed name of " Janus." Finally, at the commencement of 1871 he published under his own name the first of a number of pamphlets, by which he has gained for himself a sad renown amongst the enemies of the Church. This pamphlet, published at Prague, has the interminable title: "The Power of the Roman Popes over Princes, Countries, Peoples, and Individuals examined by the Light of their Doctrines and their Acts since the Reign of Gregory VII., to serve for the appreciation of their Infallibility, and set face to face with contradictory doctrines of the Popes and the Councils of the first Eight Centuries."

'On the appearance of this pamphlet there was a burst of admiration from all the "free-thinking" journals of Austria and imperial Germany. One Vienna newspaper, the *Press*, declared that all the attacks which had been hitherto directed against the doctrine of Infallibility were but as the prickings of a pin in comparison with the terrible blows dealt by the mace of Dr. Schulte.

'This pamphlet Mgr. Fessler thought it his duty not to leave unanswered, which gave rise to the composition of the work which is now presented to our readers.

'In this refutation the able prelate follows step by step, chapter by chapter, the reasoning of his opponent, pointing out the unfair treatment which the instruction given by the Council meets with at his hands; explaining at the same time the true doctrine, re-establishing the true import of the facts adduced, and cautioning his readers against false interpretations of them. When, with a somewhat slow, perhaps, but sure, progress he has arrived at the end of his elucidations, he draws his inevitable conclusions, and of this whole work of Dr. Schulte there remains—NOTHING.

'Dr. Schulte had asserted that the definition of the Infallibility of the Pope has completely altered the relations between the spiritual and the temporal power. The object of his work was, as he says, "to show governors and governed what a Catholic is in conscience obliged to believe if he admits the Infallibility of the Pope." So he drew up from the declarations and acts of the Popes of the Middle Ages a catalogue of what he called doctrinal propositions, which he presented to his horror-stricken readers as the decisions of the Infallible teaching office of the Sovereign Pontiffs, and so, of course, since the Council of the Vatican, as Catholic dogmas. If it can be shown that all that Dr. Schulte so laboriously quotes has nothing whatever to do with Infallibility, his book is answered, and falls as a dead letter. This feat it is that Mgr. Fessler has so victoriously performed. The result of an investigation of passage after passage, quoted by Dr. Schulte, shows that they none of them can be regarded as infallible definitions on faith and morals. Accordingly, Catholics when they accept, as is their duty, the constitution of the Council on the Infallible teaching office of the Roman Pontiff, are in no wise bound to believe what Dr. Schulte asserts they are, in regard to these assumed doctrinal propositions of Popes.

'Mgr. Fessler might have confined himself to this reply. But in behalf of those of his readers who might possibly have been perplexed regarding certain acts and declarations of Popes quoted by Dr. Schulte, although those acts and declarations do not constitute an object of the Catholic faith, the prudent Bishop has not neglected to indicate in a few short remarks at the end of his work the principal points of view, from which a right appreciation of these acts, &c., may best be obtained. Such in the abstract is the work of Mgr. Fessler, in which he has refuted by anticipation the theories which, with so much assurance, M. de Bismarck brought before his audience in the discourse which he pronounced in the Prussian Upper House on the 10th of March last, 1873. Important documents well known in France, the collective declaration of the German Bishops of May 1871, the "Pastoral Instruction" of the Swiss Bishops, have already set the principles drawn out in form by Mgr. Fessler before the eyes of such of my readers who are not theologians. People have seen in a general way how these principles have to be applied to Bulls and other Papal documents, of which the adversaries of Infallibility endeavour to avail themselves. But the great advantage of this work of Mgr. Fessler, and that which gives it a particular interest, is the application this author makes of these principles to such numerous examples. All that the adversaries of the doctrine have drawn from history in order to assail it has furnished the illustrious prelate with the opportunity of placing these very facts in their true light. Thus has he been able to show to men of good-will, but hitherto imperfectly instructed in the matter, that the doctrine against which their understanding rebelled is not the true Infallibility defined by the Council of the Vatican, but the creation of ignorance and of passion—in fact, "a false Infallibility."'

With these concluding words of the distinguished editor of the *Français* the work of Bishop Fessler is presented to the reader, in the hope that he will derive the same comfort and edification which it has afforded to many others.

AMBROSE ST. JOHN,
OF THE ORATORY.

Edgbaston, Jan. 10, 1875.

NOTE. The Translator is alone responsible for the correctness of the headings of the pages.

AUTHOR'S PREFACE

TO THE THIRD EDITION.

WHEN the publisher, a few weeks after the appearance of the first edition of my answer to Dr. Schulte, brought me the information that a second edition was required, and at the same time inquired of me whether I wished to alter anything, I told him I knew of nothing I wished to alter except a few misprints and particular words.

Since then, however, there has appeared a second enlarged edition of the work of Dr. Schulte, but as no notice was taken in it of my reply, this must be, I suppose, because both works were passing through the press at the same time. Dr. Schulte has made several additions to his second edition, which for the most part are only directed to confirm or enlarge the ground of the assertions he has made in his first.

There are, however, some new doctrinal statements of Popes, discovered by him and added in this second edition, which for the careful reader of my answer to his first work require no further refutation, since, at least according to the principles laid down by me in my answer, and which are not disputed by either side, they cannot be regarded as *ex cathedrâ* utterances, and accordingly do not belong to the subject in hand. I mention, by way of example of such new Papal doctrinal statements,

'The Pope has the right to determine for persons how they ought to dress' (p. 64 of Dr. S.'s work); and more strange still, 'That in religious questions according to the teaching of Pope Leo the Great, the Emperor is infallible' (p. 111 of his work). The latter assertion appeared to me certainly a trifle somewhat too scandalous, and to the honour of this great Pope I thought that I ought to go into the proofs of this wonderful assertion. But in a lucky moment I perceived that Dr. Schulte did not mean his words to be taken in earnest, and that he only wished to show what strange things on the subject of Infallibility might be deduced from the misunderstood or misinterpreted words of ancient writers, when people choose to interpret them in a passionate and irrational way. This, I say, broke upon me, and so I renounced my intention, and I am satisfied now to regard the statement that in religious questions, according to the doctrine of Pope Leo the Great, the Emperor is infallible, as an historical curiosity, which it would be as superfluous for me to refute, as it would be wearisome to the reader for me to attempt. One utterance of this holy Pope I will not, however, omit, and it struck me, on a fresh perusal of his letters, as very appropriate here. He says, 'Veræ fidei sufficit scire, quis doceat,'—'For the true faith it is enough to know *who* is the teacher.' But then he is not here speaking of the Emperor, but of the Pope and the Bishops.

But if the second edition of the pamphlet of Dr. Schulte has given occasion to no alterations in this third edition of my own work, the remarks of some others have reached me which will afford me the opportunity I desire, both of illustrating and of

Preface. 3

defending the position I have taken in my pamphlet. A Vienna reviewer, amidst some cavils which have no great point in them, thus expresses himself: 'The sum and substance of the matter on which, according to Schulte all depends, is the question " Whether the dogma of Papal Infallibility really reaches to that extent which he assigns to it?" The principle here involved Fessler does not contest with his opponent; he admits that not only all future but all earlier utterances of Popes, if they have been made *ex cathedrâ* in the sense already explained, have a claim to the privilege of Infallibility.'

This is true, of course; but then what this reviewer designates as the bone of contention between myself and Dr. Schulte, and wherein he says I admit Dr. Schulte's 'principle,' is really no question or bone of contention at all between us. On this point the supporters as well as the adversaries of Papal Infallibility are agreed, viz. that the definition upon the Infallible teaching office of the Roman Pontiff comprehends all former as well as all future Popes. No one whatever in the Vatican Council has been guilty of the theological absurdity of wishing to define that only Pius IX. and his successors were infallible, to the exclusion of all former Popes. The question at issue is quite of a different kind. It is whether the definition *de fide* of the Vatican Council upon the Infallible teaching office of the Roman Pontiff extends to all the different expressions which a Pope may ever casually have uttered, either as Briefs or otherwise, and even to acts of the Popes; or whether this *de fide* definition extends solely to those utterances of Popes in past as well as future times, wherein all the notes, prescribed as belonging to definition on matters of faith, combine, so as to create an infallible Papal *de fide* definition. This is the question, and in the solution of this I cannot concede an iota to Dr. Schulte, because I have learnt in the Catholic Church not to explain away (*deuteln*) a definition of a General Council (as an Augsburg reviewer unjustly says I do), but to hold to it exactly and with all my strength, TO ADD NOTHING TO IT, but at the same time to DETRACT NOTHING FROM IT. This is the position I assume in this work of mine, this is the gist of the question between me and my opponents.

The same reviewer as he proceeds in his remarks is guilty of making a certain mischievous confusion and perversion of theological ideas, which he hides behind expressions quite foreign to the subject. He says: 'The one, Fessler, draws his proofs according to mere theory; the other, Schulte, deals simply and solely with the practical historical point of view;' and he adds, 'the only real contest between the two lies in the purely theoretical treatment of Infallibility, and in its practical application.' To treat the matter in this way is simply to misunderstand the real point at issue, for what the reviewer calls 'practical application' really means that straightforward obedience and true submission which a Catholic ought to pay to the directions and definitions of the Pope.

But it was not the Vatican Council that first introduced this idea of obedience and submission. This obligation has existed time out of mind in the Catholic Church, and follows from the very nature of the Primacy. That, however, which *was* defined in the Vatican Council is another matter altogether, and it is this: that the doctrinal decisions of the Pope upon faith and morals, provided with all those notes which were prescribed in the well-weighed definition of the Council, are free from error. This definition of the Council has indeed its theoretical, as well as its practical side: the theoretical asserts that such doctrinal decisions of the Pope, made through God's assistance, are free from error; the practical side requires that every Catholic should, with a full conviction of their perfect and certain truth, devoutly accept them with that faith which belongs to truth revealed by God, and deposited in His Holy Church. I may spare myself the trouble of a longer exposition of this distinction which has its basis in theology, since the learned Bishop of Paderborn, Conrad Martin, has explained it so clearly and systematically in his work, *The true Meaning of the Vatican Definition on the Infallible Teaching Office of the Pope* (Paderborn, 1871).

An Augsburg reviewer takes objection to my expression: 'It is by no means an established fact amongst Catholic theologians, that the Syllabus with its eighty propositions belongs to those definitions of doctrine which are to be characterised as infallible;' and is of opinion that in saying this I show that the notes cannot be relied on, which I have given to make it plain how an utterance of the Pope may be recognised as *ex cathedrâ*. I, on the contrary, find that in this case, as in a hundred others, we can fully rely on the notes which have been given, for they are really good and sound notes, but yet, notwithstanding this, the application of these notes to particular cases may have its difficulties. It is the business of the science of theology to support the different views which may be taken of this question by such arguments as it has at its command, and probably in this way to bring it to pass that the right view should become the generally received view.

Should this not take place, then the authoritative decision on the matter may at any time follow. Before the Vatican Council was summoned, a Catholic was bound to pay obedience and submission to the Syllabus; nor has the Vatican Council in any respects altered this conscientious obligation. The only question which could arise was, whether the Syllabus possesses those notes on the face of it, which, according to the doctrinal definition of the fourth session of the said Council, belong to an utterance of the Pope *ex cathedrâ*.

The 'Syllabus,' as its title shows, is nothing but a collection of those errors of the age that we live in, which Pope Pius in earlier Rescripts of different dates has declared to be errors, and which accordingly he has condemned. The condemnation of errors, according to the traditional practice of the Church, is made in various forms: sometimes they are condemned as heretical; sometimes as savouring of heresy; sometimes as schismatic; sometimes simply as erroneous, or false; sometimes as dangerous, or scandalous, or perverse; sometimes as leading to heresy, or to schism, or to disobedience to ecclesiastical superiors. When a particular doctrine has been condemned by the Pope as heretical in the way designated by the doctrinal definition of the Vatican Council, speaking of the Infallible teaching office of the Pope;—then, indeed, there can be no doubt that we have under these circumstances an utterance of the Pope *ex cathedrâ*. But as in the Syllabus, through the whole catalogue of eighty propositions, designated generally in the title as 'Errors' (*Syllabus errorum*), there is nothing to show, as was pointed out above, under what category of condemned propositions, according to old ecclesiastical usage, a particular error falls, we are compelled to have recourse to the records or sources, in which the particular propositions of the Syllabus have been on previous occasions condemned by Popes, in order to learn whether it is condemned simply as erroneous, or whether it has some other designation, and notably whether it has been condemned as heretical.

The Augsburg reviewer further remarks, that whilst I blame Dr. Schulte for picking out the mere words of the definition, when he quotes the doctrinal definition of the Vatican Council on the subject of the Infallible teaching office of the Pope, and excluding the introduction and the reason for the definition, I complain of him further on, for printing the *whole* of the Bull *Unam Sanctam*. As it is here laid to me that I am acting inconsistently, I must defend myself from this charge. What it seemed to me I had a right to require of Dr. Schulte as an author was, that he should treat alike the dogmatic definition of the Vatican Council, and the Papal Constitution *Unam Sanctam*, by doing as I had done myself, viz. by pointing out that in both cases the definition *de fide* really commences after the solemn formula *definimus*; that in both the introduction was very important, not however that it was to be looked upon as the definition itself. Nor can I ever think it right that Dr. Schulte should leave out and pass *sub silentio* the introduction to the decree of the Vatican Council, calculated as it is to quiet people's minds, and, on the other hand, give entire the introduction of the Bull *Unam Sanctam*, this introduction being of a character to disquiet people; and what is still more unjustifiable, that he should treat this introduction as a doctrinal definition. And I think I have good reason to express my dissatisfaction at a proceeding, the sole object of which was to increase prejudices which were already at work, and to create a sensation in people's minds; surely a very unjustifiable proceeding, when the position a man assumes is that of one who is engaged in an impartial scientific investigation.

Another reviewer objects to my statement, that the Bull of Paul IV., *Cum ex Apostolatus officio*, of Feb. 15, 1559, is not a doctrinal definition, not an utterance of the Pope *ex cathedrâ*, but merely a disciplinary statute, and he adds that my proof of this is nothing but the title of the Bull; so he concludes: 'According to this theory it is not the contents of a Rescript, but the whim of the rubrical commentator upon it, that has to decide upon the right of a Papal Bull to be considered as an *ex cathedrâ* utterance, and thus to determine the gravest questions of conscience! Miserable subterfuge!'

Here I must be allowed, in a few words, to throw some light upon this passage of my critic, in order to show up his dishonest way of conducting a controversy. He says that I bring forward nothing but the title of the Bull in the *Bullarium*, 'so that it is not the contents of the Bull but the whim of the rubrical commentator which has to decide upon the properties of a Papal Bull;' and he permits himself to bewail my 'miserable subterfuge.' What I really said was, p. 73, 'This title, which gives a true account of its contents, is of itself enough,' &c. No one surely could direct attention to the contents of the Bull in question more plainly and definitely than I did in these words; but at the same time, to make it quite clear to my readers that the Bull really is a penal enactment, the following words out of the contents of the Bull itself will not be out of place here. Sec. 2 of the Bull says: 'Habita cum S.R.E. Cardinalibus deliberatione matura, de eorum consilio et unanimi assensu omnes et singulas excommunicationis, suspensionis, et interdicti, ac privationis, et quasvis alias sententias, censuras et pœnas a quibusvis Romanis Pontificibus prædecessoribus nostris, aut pro talibus habitis, etiam per eorum literas extravagantes, seu sacris Conciliis ab Ecclesia Dei receptis, vel Sanctorum Patrum decretis et statutis, aut sacris Canonibus ac Constitutionibus et Ordinationibus Apostolicis contra hæreticos aut schismaticos quomodolibet latas, et promulgatas Apostolicâ auctoritate approbamus et innovamus,' &c.*

The words of the contents of the Bull in question which I have here printed form *also* the title of this Bull, as I quoted in p. 73 of my pamphlet; this any one may easily convince himself of by comparing the words in both places. And yet it is in this very case that my opponent ventures openly to assert that I have made use of a 'miserable subterfuge' in drawing my proofs not from the contents of the Bull, but from the title alone; the fact being that I did expressly refer to the contents, and only for the sake of brevity quoted the words of the title, which were identical with the contents, instead of the contents of the Bull, which I have just given to my readers. These are the sort of opponents with whom

* *Bullar. Rom.* edit. Coquelines, Romæ, apud Mainardi, 1745, t. iv. p. i. p. 355.

one has to deal. When this same opponent of the Vatican definition further says, 'Bishop Fessler himself does not venture to deny that the Bull concerns doctrine *de moribus*,' I answer, 'The contents of this Bull concern morals certainly, if you reckon all penal enactments as doctrine *de moribus*.' Whether my opponent does so or not, I do not know. But this I do know, that mere penal enactments do not belong to the infallible doctrinal definitions *de fide et moribus*, of which the definition of the Vatican Council on the Infallible office of the Pope treats, and that this Bull of Paul IV. *is* a penal enactment and *not* a doctrinal definition. If he will take the trouble to read through the old Roman and later imperial penal enactments against heretics, he will find whence the specially designated penalties are derived to which he takes objection in this Bull of Paul IV.

When the Augsburg reviewer says in conclusion: 'It is impossible to discover from what, according to Dr. Fessler, a person is to draw the perfect removal of his apprehensions; no proof, no logical reason is presented to us that anything which a Pope solemnly enunciates, which he has had signed by the Cardinals and sent to all Bishops, may not have the weight of a definition in the sense of the Vatican Council,'—I thereupon point to the simple, literal, dogmatic, and logical explanation of the meaning of the definition of the Council in pages 41 to 47 of my pamphlet as the 'proof and logical reason' for my statement. Indeed, I know no proof which could be more complete, and no reason which could better meet all the requirements of sound logic. And up to this time this exposition of the subject has been contested by neither side.

Preface. 11

Another reviewer thinks he has discovered the following contradiction, as he calls it, in my pamphlet, because in p. 58 I assert that the well-known Brief *Multiplices inter* of Pius IX., one of the most important sources of the Syllabus, in which certain doctrines amongst others are condemned as *heretical*, is not a dogmatic definition; and yet on p. 70 I admit that it is a sure sign in theology of a dogmatic definition, if a doctrine is condemned by the Pope *as* heretical. Here I do not know that I can do better than publicly request the learned discoverer of this contradiction to be so good as to name to me one single doctrine which is declared expressly by the Pope in the Brief *Multiplices inter* to be *heretical*. If he does this, I will readily admit him to be right, but not otherwise.

Finally, to those of my readers who are anxious about the fidelity of quotations from the Holy Scriptures, I must acknowledge my obligation to give them a trifling explanation. The question concerns the words of Christ to St. Peter: 'I have prayed for thee that thy faith fail not; and do thou in turn one day strengthen thy brethren' (p. 36); upon which translation the Augsburg reviewer remarks: 'The author quotes, we know not why, the passage incorrectly, for it runs, "Do thou, when thou hast converted thyself, strengthen," &c.' I will tell him why I quoted this passage as I did. I did so because, following Dr. Schulte, I made use of Dr. Molitor's translation of the 'Dogmatic Constitution upon the Church of Christ' without alteration, as the attentive reader will have already observed from my pamphlet itself, where I expressly said so, and because this translation of Dr. Molitor gives this passage as it appears in my work, p. 36. The reviewer may see the reasons why this passage is so translated by consulting those commentators on Scripture who have paid particular attention to the Hebrew modes of speech.

THE

TRUE AND THE FALSE INFALLIBILITY
OF THE POPES.

WHEN a man, who for a course of years has passed for a true son of the Catholic Church and a zealous defender of her rights, suddenly turns against the Pope and Bishops with the sharpest weapons he can command, no one can deny that this is a painful sight for every one who loves his Church. Enemies of the Church will, indeed, rejoice, and eagerly greet his accession to their own ranks. Such a man is Dr. Schulte, Professor of Canon and German Law at the University of Prague, who has just published a pamphlet with this high-sounding title, 'The Power of the Roman Pontiffs over Sovereigns, Countries, Peoples, Individuals, according to their Doctrines and Acts, held up to the Light, in order to afford persons the means of making a true estimate of their claim to Infallibility.' Misleading indeed is the light this pamphlet holds up for our guidance, the subject being really presented to our view in a light wholly false and extremely repulsive. Surely love of truth imperatively requires that so grave a subject should at any rate be represented in its just and fair light; and this is the object the author of the following pages has set before himself, viz. to present the subject to his readers, without passion and without partiality, with that knowledge which many years' study, and an exact acquaintance with facts and circumstances, enable him to do.

The subject, as treated by Dr. Schulte, is divided into the following heads:

I. 'Exposition of the subject as introduction.'

II. 'The contents of the definition of the Vatican Council, "On the Infallible teaching Office of the Roman Pontiff."'

III. *Part* 1.—'Doctrinal propositions of Popes simply *ex cathedrâ*, and their acts in relation to states, countries, peoples, and individuals.'

III. *Part* 2.—Relations of Popes to the state-law. Treatment of heretics.*

IV. 'Pleas devised to quiet the conscience, and their confutation.'

V. 'Considerations on the law of the state.'†

* This division, being made for the convenience of English readers, is given in the words of the Translator.

† It must be borne in mind that the headings of the chapters are all taken from Dr. Schulte's pamphlet; if not in his own words, at least in their substance. TRANSLATOR.

CHAPTER I.

'EXPOSITION OF THE SUBJECT AS INTRODUCTION.'

1. THE general exposition of the subject with which my opponent, Dr. Schulte, opens his attack upon the Church commences with a German translation of the Address of several of our archbishops and bishops, issued under the date of April 10, 1870.* This Address entreats the President of the General Congregation of the Council not to bring on for consideration, or to decide the question of the Infallibility of the Pope, before the question as to the power of the Holy See in temporal matters, or rather, as to the relative position of the ecclesiastical and political power, has been thoroughly weighed in all its bearings, and put to the test. These prelates, it seems, thought it desirable that the question whether Christ our Lord had given to St. Peter and his successors the power over kings and realms should *first* be laid before the Council, and thus that the relation of the ecclesiastical to the temporal power should first be made matter of mature deliberation. He adds himself that this Address produced no result.

Accordingly, this Address of certain archbishops and bishops is at once the shield or bulwark behind which Dr. Schulte shelters himself, and the ground on which he rests, in order to open his attack upon the Pope. The Bishops to whom he refers

* I ought to say that with respect to this Address of April 10, 1870, I have not had at hand any copy of it, except the translation of Dr. Schulte himself, which he assures us is perfectly correct.

having acknowledged it to be the principal task of the Council 'to advance in the best way possible the greater glory of God, and the welfare of mankind in general,' find it natural that in so great a body of men different opinions should arise—not, however, so different as to split them up into parties. Accordingly, out of the various difficulties presenting themselves in the consideration of the question of Papal Infallibility, they make particular mention of a specially weighty one, and this, their Address says, is a difficulty which directly touches the relationship of Catholic doctrine to civil society; in the treatment of which subject some contradiction might be expected to arise between the doctrine hitherto taught by them on the relationship between Church and State, and the conclusions which might follow from the doctrine of the Infallibility of the Pope.

Well, it is a matter of fact that this difficulty was not separately considered, and it is also matter of fact that, in the matters treated of in the Council, the relations of Church and State power did not come first under consideration, but the doctrine respecting the Pope as the Foundation and visible Head of the Catholic Church. Whoever will look at the question without prejudice will see that there are clearly two different ways of viewing it—viz. first, whether it is best to commence with the Catholic doctrine respecting the Pope as the Foundation and visible Head of the Catholic Church, and then *afterwards* with the doctrine respecting the relations between Church and State, or *vice versâ;* that reasons can be alleged on both sides; and that the view that the doctrine respecting the Pope ought to take precedence is, at any rate, a well-grounded one.

But it may be said that, had this question of the relations of Church and State taken the precedence, difficulties touching the Infallibility of the Pope would have then been examined. No doubt they would; and so they have been now, though not exactly in the form in which one portion of the Council wished and required. The discussion, which continued for many weeks, in which bishops of all countries took part, had this very object in view— viz. to throw all possible light on the subject when considered on every side.

But, continues Dr. Schulte, 'anyhow these difficulties have not all been properly solved.'

To this I answer: If before doctrinal matters were decided in the Catholic Church, we had always had to wait until all difficulties were cleared away, General Councils would have had a long time to wait. When the Council of Nicæa declared that the doctrine, 'The Son of God is very God,' was a dogma of the faith, all difficulties were so far from being cleared away, that during four whole centuries, in which period flourished the greatest teachers of doctrine the world has ever known—Athanasius, Hilary, Basil, Ambrose—those theologians had to put forth their whole strength in order to solve these difficulties. This has been the case with subsequent General Councils; and it is the excellent and all-important task of the science of theology, after the authority of the teaching Church has solemnly and formally declared the truth revealed by God, to solve the difficulties which present themselves in respect of each particular doctrine, to aid every man to acknowledge the truth himself, and to help to obtain a victory for that truth in the world at large. After each dog-

C

matic definition there have ever been found in the Catholic Church men, on the one hand, who contested the truth of the definition, and who enhanced its difficulty; and men who, on the other hand, have done their best to defend it, and who in the end have happily solved all difficulties which stood in the way of its general acceptance. The former have long since been subjected to the judgment of history and to the just judgment of God; the latter, the Catholic Church names through all ages with honour, and these, too, have had their reward with God.

2. The bishops who signed the address are, with the exception of four, not mentioned by name by Dr. Schulte. It is only said: 'It was signed by almost all the Austrian and Hungarian bishops, and by several of those German bishops who, since the Fulda pastoral of August 31, 1870, have been seeking, with a reckless arbitrary exertion of authority perfectly unintelligible, to introduce this same doctrine of the Infallibility of the Pope, so as to cause an open breach amongst Catholics.' A severe taunt this, to use towards a portion of the German bishops! to whose charge, moreover, he still further lays, that in their pastoral of 1870 they used no single word to imply that they themselves admitted the July doctrine in substance. And of these bishops he remarks: 'After they had persistently and boldly declared their *non placet* up to the decisive day of July 13, they, to their disgrace, remained absent from the formal act of July 18; and this from mere human respect of persons.'

Here I must again say: These are hard words for a man of learning to fling publicly in the faces of German, Austrian, and Hungarian archbishops and bishops—viz. that, out of mere human and personal motives, they kept away from the solemn act of expressing their assent to a revealed truth. Such a hard judgment as this neither the Pope nor their brother bishops pronounced upon them; it has been reserved for a layman to constitute himself the judge of their consciences, and to raise this cry of scorn against bishops: 'You stayed away from the solemn sitting of the Council, July 18, out of mere human respect.' What avails it to say, 'He doesn't blame them for it'? The reproach of acting in so grave a matter from a motive of mere human respect is the greatest reproach that can be made to a bishop.

Very different was the judgment of their brother bishops upon the cause of their absence. It is not in the General Congregation, but in the Solemn Session of the Council, that the decisive vote is given. This it is easy to see from the acts of General Councils. If even up to this point in the last General Congregation before the Solemn Session a bishop is not satisfied as to all his difficulties, or if he thinks it better that the decision should not yet be pronounced on such and such a doctrine, he may in the interval between the last General Congregation and the Solemn Session acquire a full conviction on the subject by discoursing with other theologians, by study of the subject, and by prayer, and may thus overcome his last difficulties, and see that it is well that the definition should be made. Nay, even if he cannot attain this full conviction and insight into the matter by any exertion of his own, he will wait for the decision of the Council with a calm trust in God, without himself taking part in it, because up to this point he lacks the necessary certainty of conviction. When, however, the Council by its decision puts an end to the matter, then at length his Catholic conscience tells him plainly what he must now think and what he must now do; for it is then that the Catholic bishop, whom hitherto unsolved difficulties have kept from participation in the public session and from the solemn voting, says: '*Now* it is undoubtedly certain that this doctrine is revealed by God, and is therefore a portion of the Catholic faith, and therefore I accept it on faith, and must now proclaim it to my clergy and people as a doctrine of the Catholic Church. The difficulties which hitherto made it hard for me to give my consent, and to the perfect solution of which I have not even yet attained, *must* be capable of a solution; and so I shall honestly busy myself with all the powers of my soul to find their solution for myself and for those whose instruction God has confided to my care.' Then those bishops who in the last General Congregation voted with the *non placets*, only because they really thought it was not a good thing, not necessary, not for the benefit of souls in countries well known to them, and who for this reason abstained from taking part in this decision, may, after the solemn decision, if they think it advisable, represent to the faithful of their dioceses the position which they previously adopted towards the doctrine, in order that their conduct may not be misunderstood. But they must now themselves unhesitatingly accept the doctrine which has been decided, and make it known to their people in its true and proper bearings, without reserve, and in such manner that the injurious effects which they themselves apprehended may be as much as possible obviated and removed; for it is not permitted to the bishop, as the divinely-appointed teacher of the clergy and people, to be silent about or to withhold a doctrine of the Faith revealed by God, because he apprehends or thinks that some may take offence at it. Nay, rather it is his business so prudently to bring it about in the declaration of that doctrine, that its true sense and import may hereafter be clearly represented, all erroneous misrepresentations of it be excluded, the reasons for the decision of the doctrine brought out plainly, and all objections to it zealously met and answered.

And this was what the German bishops really did think, and do. In proof whereof I will venture to mention the name of the Archbishop of Cologne, who thus speaks: ' In respect of this doctrine, I, in common with many other bishops and laymen, although I have always given my assent to its truth, nevertheless held a different opinion from the majority of bishops at the Council, and made no concealment of my opinion that the definition was inopportune in our time, and I also differed in respect of certain particulars connected with the doctrine. Since, however, after a deep and thorough investigation and examination, the question has been decided by the Ecumenical Council, in the firm conviction that every Catholic is bound to submit unconditionally his own personal view of the matter to the decisions of such a Council—the highest legitimate authority in the Church—I have dismissed all previous doubts and anxieties on the subject, and I feel myself bound here publicly to declare that I expect the same submission from every Catholic and subject of this archdiocese, as the fulfilment of a simple duty of their religion.'—*Pastoral*, September 10, 1870.*

* See note at the end of this chapter.

As to the way in which the bishops thought fit to make known to their subjects this obligation of their faith—whether it should be done by a simple printed notice in the official gazette of the diocese, as at Vienna, Prague, Leitmeritz, and elsewhere, or by a special pastoral, as at Cologne, Saltsburg, Munich, Regensburg, &c., or by a notice from the altar-rails of the church, as at Linz—is immaterial; since any one of these notifications shows sufficiently that each particular bishop looked upon this doctrine as a doctrine of the Catholic faith, and required that his subjects should do so likewise. Moreover, every one is aware that all doctrinal definitions of the Catholic Church demand a conscientious acceptation on the part of every Catholic as soon as he comes to a certain knowledge of the doctrine, and this without any special publication in a particular diocese.

3. Our opponent next insists on the great importance of an exact and thorough knowledge of History, in order completely to sift the doctrine of the infallible teaching authority of the Pope, and to ascertain what value History has set upon it. The necessity of such a knowledge we readily admit, without, however, admitting that it will at all avail the enemies of the doctrine. For it is perfectly well known to every one who is acquainted with the literary works, both old and new, which have reference to this subject, that the advocates of the doctrine of Papal Infallibility, as well as its adversaries, appeal to the history of the Church and to its sources. History experiences the same fate that has befallen Holy Scripture. The advocates, as well as the enemies, of every particular Catholic doctrine on which, in the course of ages, dogmatic definitions have been pronounced,

have always appealed to Holy Scripture. So it is with the appeal to history; but with this great difference —that we honour Holy Scripture as the divine source of our Catholic faith (though not the only source), whereas history, in so far as we consider it apart from that tradition which is one source of our faith, has only a human authority, and is amenable to the full force of the laws of sound criticism. Accordingly, history will furnish those supporters of the doctrine of the Infallibility of the Pope who wish to go to its very foundation with extremely valuable and rich materials. Those things which the adversaries of the doctrine adduce out of history, in order to assail it, will present us too with an excellent opportunity of placing in a right light what the doctrine really is, and of showing, by particular examples, in what cases it derives support from such instances, and in what cases not. These records of the past will not then be, as our adversaries taunt us, 'a very disagreeable subject for us to contemplate;' say rather they are the sources which enable us to maintain our point, and that their investigation is most desirable, since without these there can be no real history at all. And if there is anything to which the writer of these pages owes a grateful acknowledgment, it is to these very sources of his information being as exact as they are.

4. Dr. Schulte now further declares that, though a Catholic born and bred, he has never believed in Papal Infallibility, and he asserts that, as to this decree of July 18th, 1870, 'he can find no authority for it either in Scripture, or in the Fathers, or in any other sound source of historical information, as it is taught in Caps. iii. and iv. of the Vatican Council.'

Such a declaration makes it clear enough what

position he assumes, and a very deplorable position it is. He refuses to accept the definition *de fide* of an Ecumenical Council; he cares nothing for the authority of the living teaching Church; only for what he thinks he finds in Scripture, in the Fathers, and in other genuine ancient sources. This is the way to forsake the Catholic Church altogether. Every one is to follow his own guidance, his own private judgment; one finds one thing, another finds another; each calls out, 'I have found out the truth; come to me.' This is the way all errors have arisen, and it is this uncatholic position, which he has assumed, which is at the root of this particular perversion of his judgment, as is manifest from the following words he makes use of: 'As it is not my bishop or my priest who will bring me to heaven by his prayers, if I myself believe not in Christ, and live not as a Christian ought to live; so neither can I, nor any one else who wishes to know what is right, intrust my salvation to the responsibility which a third person might be willing to assume for me. Of my own self God will, in the next world, require a reckoning of my life. To the doctrine of the Apostle (Rom. xiv. 12, 2 Cor. v. 10*) I hold fast, and will never shield myself under the responsibility of any one but myself.'

When then Dr. Schulte says, 'Neither Pope, nor bishop, nor parish priest, can bring me to heaven by his prayers, if I live not as a Christian and believe in Christ,' no doubt he states perfectly correctly that no

---

* I give these passages that the reader may judge how far they help Dr. Schulte's cause: Rom. xiv. 12—'Every one of us shall render an account to God for himself;' 2 Cor. v. 10—'For we must all be manifested before the judgment seat of Christ, that every one may receive the proper things of the body according as he hath done, whether it be good or evil.'

one goes to heaven by another's prayers, if he does not believe in Christ and live according to his faith. When, however, he adds, 'Just as little can I, or any one who wishes to know what is right, trust my salvation to the responsibility which a third person may be willing to assume,' this is a proposition with a double sense, one of which senses is true, and the other false. It is perfectly true, if it is a question of the transgression of a law which I may have had the misfortune to commit, which transgression a third person may, perhaps, say he will take upon his own shoulders; as if a person were to say, 'If you commit such and such a murder, such and such an adultery, such and such a theft, such and such an act of fraud, I will take upon myself the responsibility of the deed.' In such matters assuredly the responsibility which another person takes upon himself, will in no wise avail me before God. In this sense, then, the proposition is true. But if any one wishes to extend the application of this proposition, so as to say that I must not accept a Catholic doctrine on faith when the teaching Church declares it to be of faith, because I myself do not find the doctrine in Scripture, the Fathers, or other genuine ancient sources of Church doctrine, then this proposition is used in a false sense, by the substitution of the act of the individual's subjective belief for the objective truth declared by the Church, which truth is based upon the infallible teaching office of the holy Catholic Church. What an amazing difference, then, is there between these two propositions! In the one case, a man offers to bear for another the consequences of an act of every-day life, be it of belief or unbelief, be it of a good or bad action, and, in the other case, a Catholic Christian, relying on the authority of the teaching Church, on which God has Himself taught him to rely, 'he that heareth you heareth Me,' accepts a doctrine as a truth revealed by God, because the teaching Church, under the special guidance of the Holy Spirit, has declared it to be so. If a man is not to be required to believe such a declaration as this, then all difference between an infallibly teaching Catholic Church and Protestantism in all its forms, with the unlimited right of private judgment, is at an end. Assuredly he says truly, 'God will some time call every one to a reckoning for his conduct during life.' Certainly He will call our once-Catholic opponent, and will say to him, 'I gave you the grace to be born and bred up in the Catholic Church; you both might have learnt and you ought to have learnt that there resides in the Catholic Church an infallible teaching authority, to which, in matters of faith, every Catholic is bound to submit. From the man who rebels against that authority and rejects her decision will I demand an account, and an account twofold and threefold more severe from him who, in his capacity of public teacher, misleads from the Faith the youth who have been intrusted to him, and causes them to rebel against the authority of the Church, and who, for this reason, will have the guilt of the shipwreck of those souls on his conscience.'

5. Having assumed, as I have described, so fearfully mistaken a position, our opponent proceeds to assert that he himself preserves and holds fast the faith of the Fathers and the teaching of the ancient Catholic Church in rejecting the decision of the Vatican Council on Papal Infallibility, (the July Constitution, as he is pleased to call it). Well then, the Vatican Council has solemnly spoken, and

said that 'holding fast to the tradition of the Christian faith, which it has received from the beginning,' it declares this to be a doctrine of the Faith. If this faith is contained in the tradition of the Christian faith, which has existed from the beginning, then must it have been the faith of the Fathers and the doctrine of the ancient Catholic Church. So here we have assertion *versus* assertion. The Vatican Council declares the doctrine of the infallible teaching office of the Roman Pope has been in the Church from the beginning, delivered down from the most ancient times; Dr. Schulte says that he, while, maintaining his own view of the question, he does not accept the doctrine, still holds fast to the faith of the Fathers and to the doctrine of the ancient Catholic Church. Whom is the world to believe? Dr. Schulte, or the Pope and the Bishops? Hardly will he have the confidence to answer, 'The world is to believe me, not the Pope and the Bishops.' Yet, according to the position he has assumed in his pamphlet, he cannot bring himself to answer, 'The world must believe not me, but the Pope and Bishops.' Accordingly, all that remains for him to say is, 'Everybody is to search for himself the Holy Scriptures and the writings of the Fathers, and examine the ancient records, in order to find out the truth for himself.'

Out of compassion for the author I decline to stigmatise with its proper name such a position as this which he has assumed; his own conscience must, when he calmly weighs the matter over, tell him what a course he has entered on, and whither such principles must naturally lead him. How utterly unreal, how completely impossible in practice, such a suggestion is, my readers will easily see, if they do but consider that they are thus, every one of them, required to examine Holy Scripture, the Fathers, and the ancient records of the Church, in order to know what they have to believe respecting the infallible teaching office of the Roman Pontiff; whether, having made such an investigation, they are compelled to accept this doctrine as a doctrine of the Catholic faith, and under what limitations. In order, however, to prevent any one misunderstanding my meaning, I think it right to remark, that in contesting the position of Dr. Schulte, as regards the duty of every one to examine Scripture, the Fathers, and the ancient records for himself, I am far from dissuading an examination of them as a thing objectionable in itself. On the contrary, I highly value such an investigation, and I hold it to be a very right and proper thing to make it, when it is done in a right manner. If, however, this examination is praised and recommended in order to represent the solemn definition of the teaching Church as an error, then will a thing that is good in itself, instead of being a means of establishing and defending the truth, only serve as a battering-ram against that truth. This is a bad and objectionable proceeding.

6. One other assertion of our opponent needs to be cleared up. It is this: he says, 'The Church is not founded that the Hierarchy may govern, and the laity obey; but the Lord hath founded His Church that every one may find in her the safe way to work out his own salvation.' As this assertion here meets the eye, it presents to our view a truth—viz. that the final cause of the foundation of the Church was not that the Hierarchy might govern, and that the laity might obey, but that every one might find salvation in her. But if this assertion is made to repre-

sent as a fact that it is not the will of God, in the foundation of His Church, that the Pope and the Bishops should instruct and govern His holy Church, and that the laity should listen to them in the Church, then is this a great misrepresentation of the truth. When, however, I say it is the will of God that the Pope and the Bishops should instruct and govern the Church, of course I mean to say this in that ordinary sense in which the words have ever been understood, and the thing practised in the Church. To the Pope and to the Bishops, in the person of Peter and of the rest of the Apostles, was the whole truth of Revelation committed by Jesus Christ, the Founder of the holy Church. This truth is preserved by them, with a true and earnest watchfulness, as a precious treasure intrusted to them by God, and laid up in their keeping, to be imparted, either by themselves .or by their assistants, the priests, to all who, by a true acceptance of this truth and by Baptism, have either already found admission into her, or who shall hereafter find admission. This is what the Pope and the Bishops, according to the will of God, teach. But it is also the will of God that they should govern the Church. This means that they should lead on their way to heaven the faithful committed to their pastoral care by means of the truth which they have received, as also by the means of grace which they have received to administer, and by virtue of that spiritual power with which, in the third place, they are endowed. This they know right well, and bear it always in mind: that in their ministrations they should always, and before all things, as their first duty, follow the example of their Divine Redeemer, the first and highest

Pastor of souls, who hath said to them, 'I have given you an example, that you also should do as I have done unto you.' 'Learn of Me, for I am meek and lowly of heart.' 'He who will be great among you, let him be your servant; and he who will be first, let him be your minister, like as the Son of Man is not come to be ministered unto, but to minister and to give His life a ransom for many.' This ministration for the good of souls is exercised in very different ways: sometimes with loving and sometimes with zealous words; sometimes with instruction by word of mouth, and sometimes with words of written admonition, after the fashion of the Apostles, in the doctrine and love of Christ.

It is greatly to be regretted certainly that our opponent, Dr. Schulte, has met with so many distressing proofs of disquieted minds, as he says he has in his work, *A Glance into the State of the Church in several Dioceses.* However, I, being myself a Bishop, know the state of many Churches, and the mind of many Bishops thereon, and I am compelled to express my opinion that Dr. Schulte met with either very one-sided informants or discontented grumblers in those dioceses he visited; so that the prospect looked much more gloomy than it really was. That all regulations of this world, even when they rest on divine direction, in so far as they have to be carried out by men, are more or less subject to human imperfections, is too well known to need to be reasserted; nor can this now be denied. But we must not for this reason deny the divine supervision in the Church, set ourselves against it or prejudge it, and that falsely too. God has willed it and ordered it that in His Church Pope and Bishops should teach and govern, and that the laity should obey. If a layman rebels against the Pope or against the Bishops, because, as he says, the good of the Church is of a higher order of good than the momentary pleasure of the Hierarchy, and that he has no fear if his conscience is not alarmed, then I am compelled to make the remark that we Bishops too, and the Pope have a conscience, and that this doctrinal definition respecting the infallible teaching authority of the Roman Pontiff has been long and maturely weighed before God in prayer, and after long and earnest study has been declared with a quiet conscience; and I also declare it to be my firm belief that those Bishops who, in supplement to the Council, declared their adhesion to the doctrine, and gave their reasons in excellent pastorals, acted simply according to their own consciences. Lastly, as regards the good of the Church, which Dr. Schulte professes he thinks imperilled by the momentary perversion of the Hierarchy, I ask, who can imagine that things are come to such a pass that in this nineteenth century the Church of God has come to be betrayed by the Pope and Bishops, and that our opponent, Dr. Schulte, should be the man chosen by God to take the Church under his protection? Are, then, the Pope and Bishops so forsaken by God that He should let them sink into so dangerous an error in doctrine? Has the Lord forgotten His promises? Can He ever forget them, and give over His Church a prey to destruction?

Note to page 21.

Quite in unison with the Archbishop of Cologne are the sentiments (as they have been credibly reported to us by the public press) of the Prince Primate of Hungary, John

Simor, Archbishop of Gran, and his sentiments may be taken as expressing those of the rest of the Hungarian Bishops. We are there told that the Prince Primate never for a moment contemplated denying that the Council was ecumenical; that 'He never was opposed to the doctrine itself "that the Pope was Infallible by virtue of the promise given to the Founder of the Church," but only to the *opportuneness* of so weighty a step, fraught with such important consequences, in the present deplorable state of affairs. Besides, after that the Council, and, by the voice of the Council (as the certain and undisputed doctrine of the Church has ever held), the Holy Ghost Himself, has spoken, the Prince Primate was as little capable as any other faithful member of our Holy Church of entertaining a doubt about the validity and binding force of the Infallibility Dogma.'—*German-Hungarian Monthly Journal*, December 1870.

CHAPTER II.

'THE CONTENTS OF THE DEFINITION OF THE VATICAN COUNCIL, "ON THE INFALLIBLE TEACHING OFFICE OF THE ROMAN PONTIFF." '*

7. THIS portion of Dr. Schulte's pamphlet contains a German translation† of the words of the definition of the Vatican Council now under consideration ; it enumerates the particular propositions therein contained, and draws from them their logical and juridical consequences.

I cannot refrain here from expressing my sense of the extraordinary unfairness of the writer in quoting the definition without the reasons which the Council itself gives in express words for making the definition. This context is absolutely necessary in order that we may rightly understand so important a matter. In order to supply this deficiency, I will present to my readers, in the vernacular, the entire section or chapter 'On the Infallible Teaching Office of the Roman Pontiff,' as given by the Council. The whole section, or fourth chapter, of the first dogmatic definition on the Church of Christ runs as follows:

'*Caput Quartum.*

'ON THE INFALLIBLE TEACHING OFFICE (MAGISTERIUM) OF THE
'ROMAN PONTIFF.

'That in the apostolical primacy which the Roman Pontiff, as successor of the prince of the Apostles,

* Bear in mind the headings of the chapters are taken from Dr. Schulte's pamphlet.
† By Dr. W. Molitor, Regensburg, 1870.

D

Peter, has over the whole Church, is comprehended also the supreme teaching authority, this holy See has always firmly held, and this the constant practice of the Church confirms, and this the Ecumenical Councils have themselves declared, and above all, that Council in which the East met the West for the union of faith and charity. For the Fathers of the Fourth Council of Constantinople, treading in the footsteps of their forefathers, made the following solemn confession: "The first condition of salvation is to keep the rule of sound faith. And as the declaration uttered by our Lord Jesus Christ can never fail,* when He says, 'Thou art Peter, and upon this Rock I will build My Church,' so have the words there said actually come to pass, forasmuch as in the apostolical chair the Catholic faith has ever remained inviolate and its holy doctrine been celebrated. Desiring to be in no wise separated from its faith and doctrine, we hope to be made worthy to be in that one communion which the Apostolic See declares, wherein resides the perfect and true wholeness of the Christian religion."† With the acquiescence of the Second Council of Lyons the Greeks made this confession: "That the holy Roman Church possesses the highest and the full primacy and principality over the whole Catholic Church, which it truly and humbly acknowledges it has received from our Lord Himself in the person of St. Peter, the prince and chief of the Apostles,

* 'Prætermitti,' used with 'jus,' in the sense of 'being brought to naught.' See *Facciolati in verbo.* TRANSLATOR.

† From a formula of Pope Hormisdas, as it was proposed by Adrian II. to the Eighth Ecumenical Council, viz. the Fourth Council of Constantinople, and was signed by the Fathers there assembled.

together with the fulness of power; and as this Church is before all other Churches bound to defend the truth of the faith, so ought all questions of faith which may at any time arise to be decided according to her judgment." The Council of Florence finally defined: "That the Roman Pontiff, the true Vicar of Christ, is the head of the whole Church and the Father and Doctor of all Christians, and that to him, in St. Peter, was committed by our Lord Jesus Christ the full power to feed the universal Church, to rule, and to guide it."

'In order to fulfil this pastoral office, our Predecessors have, time after time, directed their unwearied labours that the wholesome doctrine of Christ might be spread abroad among all people of the earth, and with like care have they watched that, wherever the true doctrine has been received, there it should be preserved pure and undefiled. Therefore have the Bishops of the whole world, sometimes individually, and sometimes assembled in solemn synods, acting according to the long-received custom of the Church, and according to the pattern of the ancient rule, brought before this apostolic chair those difficulties which were ever arising in matters of faith, in order that the rents in faith might there be mended, where alone the faith could never fail.* The Roman Pontiffs, however, have, as times and circumstances warranted, —sometimes by summoning Ecumenical Councils or by asking the opinion of the Church throughout the world, sometimes by particular synods, sometimes by the use of other means which Divine Providence put in their way,—defined that those things should be held firm which they had thus learnt, under God's

* St. Bernard, Epis. 190.

assistance, to be in accordance with Holy Scripture and apostolical traditions. For the Holy Spirit was not promised to the successors of St. Peter, that by His revelation they might make known a new doctrine, but that by His assistance they might holily preserve and faithfully expound the revelation delivered to the Apostles, or, in other words, the "deposit of the faith" (*depositum fidei*). This is that apostolical doctrine which all the venerable Fathers of the Church have embraced, and all the orthodox holy Doctors have venerated and followed; for they had the most perfect conviction that this holy See of Peter always remains free from all error, according to the divine promise of our Lord and Saviour, which He made to the prince of His disciples: "I have prayed for thee, that thy faith fail not; and thou, in thy turn one day,[*] strengthen thy brethren."

'This gracious gift of the truth and of indefectible faith has been accordingly given by God to Peter and his successors in this See, that they might discharge their high office to the salvation of all; that so the universal flock of Christ, turned from the poisonous allurements of error, might be nourished by the pasture of heavenly doctrine ; so that, all occasion of schism having been removed, the whole Church might be preserved in unity, and, resting on its own solid basis, might stand fast against the gates of hell.

'But as at this present time, when the wholesome efficacy of the apostolic office is most pressingly needed, there are found not a few who derogate from its dignity, We esteem it quite necessary solemnly to assert the prerogative which the Only-

[*] See the author's Preface, concluding paragraph.

begotten Son of God has graciously declared to be bound up with the highest pastoral authority.*

'Whilst, then, We remain firm to the tradition of the Christian faith, which has come down to us from the beginning, We teach, in accordance with this holy Council, to the glory of God our Saviour, to the exaltation of the Catholic religion, and for the benefit of all Christian people, and declare it to be a doctrine revealed by God, that the Roman Pontiff, when he speaks from his chair of teaching (*ex cathedrâ*)—that is to say, when he, in the exercise of his office as pastor and doctor of all Christians, by virtue of his supreme apostolic power, defines a doctrine on faith or morals as to be held by the universal Church, by virtue of the divine assistance promised to him in St. Peter—possesses that Infallibility with which the Divine Redeemer willed His Church to be furnished in the definition of a doctrine respecting faith or morals; and that therefore such definitions of the Roman Pontiff are of themselves, and not merely when they have received the consent of the Church, unalterable. Should, then, any one—which God forbid!—venture to contest this definition of Ours, let him be Anathema.'

8. It can hardly escape the observation of any one who peruses this fourth chapter of the Council thoroughly and carefully, that the reasons given for the definition and the historical account of the doctrine are of immense importance for a right understanding of the matter. It was, then, very unfair of

---

* All this, from the beginning of this chapter up to this point, Dr. Schulte has omitted, and has only admitted into his article the passage commencing 'Whilst, then.'

Dr. Schulte, to say the least, to extract from the chapter on Infallibility the bare words of the definition, and by so doing to leave the readers of his pamphlet in entire ignorance of all that important matter which, with the best intentions, the Council itself had given as the reasons for the definition, and, in order to forestall misunderstandings, had placed in close connection with the definition itself.

I have, therefore, thought it especially necessary to give my readers the words at full length which the Vatican Council made use of in declaring its mind on the infallible teaching office of the Roman Pontiff; and I beg my readers to pay particular attention to this context of the definition as regards the present controversy.

The very title of the chapter is remarkable. It runs (in order to designate precisely the subject which is under consideration), 'On the Infallible Teaching Office of the Roman Pontiff.' This expression, 'on the Infallible teaching office,' was chosen purposely, instead of the title 'On the Infallibility,' in order to forestall the erroneous deductions which might be drawn from the general term 'Infallibility' by those who were disposed to dispute the doctrine on this very ground—viz. because it was so general. Such persons would be sure to misrepresent the doctrine to others, and mislead them in their inquiries. Accordingly, the Council carefully and exactly declared, by the very title, in what respect the term 'infallible' is used of the Roman Pontiff.

The contents of the chapter 'On the Infallible teaching office of the Roman Pontiff' may be concisely viewed and readily stated in its principal features as follows:

It is the ancient consistent doctrine of the Church, says the Pope, that to the Roman Pontiff is given by God the supreme power in the Church, in order always to preserve its unity. But in this supreme power is contained the supreme teaching power, as the Church has always acknowledged in General Councils of ancient times, and especially in the Fourth Council of Constantinople (A.D. 869), in the Second Council of Lyons (A.D. 1274), and in the Council of Florence (A.D. 1439). He also shows how the Popes acted when difficult questions relating to faith were, according to ancient custom and prescription, laid before the Apostolical See for decision by the Bishops, viz. either, by assembling the Bishops in Ecumenical Council; or by inquiring into and obtaining the knowledge in some other way of what the general feeling of the universal Church was upon such and such a point; or by summoning particular synods; and, lastly, by using all such means as Divine Providence put in their power. And with this assistance the Popes decided that doctrine to be revealed by God, and accordingly to be held by all as *de fide*, which they, with God's assistance, recognised as conformable to Holy Scripture and the apostolical traditions; always themselves holily preserving and truly interpreting, by the same divine assistance, the *depositum fidei* preserved in the Church. This apostolical teaching of the Popes, he says, the venerable Fathers and all orthodox teachers in the Church have, from of old up to the present time, accepted with a full and perfect conviction that the See of blessed Peter, by virtue of the Divine Providence of our Lord and Saviour, has been constantly kept from all error; for so Jesus Christ spoke to Peter: 'I have prayed for thee, that thy faith fail not; and do thou, in thy turn one day, strengthen thy brethren' (Luc. cap. xxii. v. 32). The reason is also added why God gave this great grace to St. Peter and his successors in the office of supreme teacher—viz. that they might exercise this office for the spiritual benefit of all the faithful, that thereby the Church, trusted by God to their supreme pastoral care, might through those who exercise this office of supreme teacher be maintained without fear of error in the divine truth, and thus the whole Church be preserved in unity. Therefore, in accordance with that tradition which has ever existed in the Church from the beginning of the Christian religion, and which has always been maintained inviolate, it is declared by the Vatican Council, to the glory of God and for the salvation of Christian people, to be a constituent part of that Catholic faith revealed by God, 'that the Roman Pontiff, when he speaks from his chair of teaching, (or *ex cathedrâ*)— that is to say, when he, in the exercise of his office as pastor and doctor of all Christians, by virtue of his supreme apostolic authority, defines a doctrine which concerns faith or morals to be held *de fide* by the whole Church—does, by reason of the divine assistance promised to him in the person of St. Peter, possess that Infallibility with which the Divine Redeemer willed His Church to be provided in the decision of matters respecting faith or morals; and that accordingly all such definitions of the Roman Pontiff are of themselves, and not then only when they have received the consent of the Church, unalterable.'

Having thus supplied, in the little review we have made, the gap left by Dr. Schulte, by giving the important introduction to the definition of the

Vatican Council on the Infallible teaching office of the Roman Pontiff, and shown also the principal motives by which this Council was actuated, we are confident that it will be clear to all unprejudiced persons that 'the decisive passage' (as Dr. Schulte calls it, and which alone he quotes in his pamphlet, from the end of the chapter) will produce a very different impression, if considered in connection with the reasons which the Council itself assigns for the definition, and in connection also with the historical explanation, from that which it would produce, if viewed wrenched out of its context, and isolated. They will now be able to see how this supreme and infallible office has *hitherto* been exercised by the Popes, and from this they will judge how it *will be* exercised in future. And I must say it is a most disingenuous commencement of Dr. Schulte in his pamphlet, that he has torn off from the words of the Definition the Council's reasons for it, and its historical explanation in this chapter of the Vatican Council 'On the Infallible teaching office of the Roman Pontiff.'

9. I admit, however, the 'decisive passage' itself does require some remarks to enable persons thereby thoroughly to understand it; for it is with this passage that Dr. Schulte commences that erroneous exposition of the Vatican definition, which I have undertaken to examine and refute; it becomes then my duty to open out and disclose the sources of his erroneous view and his misrepresentations; and this I can best do by explaining at once what is the right sense of the definition, and so letting every one see when and where the author of the pamphlet under examination has deviated from the path of truth.

The definition asserts that the Roman Pontiff, by

virtue of the divine assistance, possesses the Infallibility promised to the Church in his doctrinal teaching only when he speaks *ex cathedrâ*. This is the expression used for centuries, and for that very reason preserved in speaking of definitions of the faith.

But as this expression *ex cathedrâ*—or, Anglice, 'to speak from the chair of teaching'—is not generally intelligible, as it is a technical expression drawn from theological science, the Council itself added a short explanation of it. It says it means, ' When he (*i.e.* the Pope), in the exercise of his teaching office as pastor and instructor (*doctor*) of all the faithful, by virtue of his highest apostolical power, defines, as to be held by the whole Church, doctrine that regards faith or morals.'*

(1) By this expression, then, *ex cathedrâ*, the gift of God's divine grace conveying Infallibility in faith and morals to the Roman Pontiff, the visible head of the Catholic Church, and who in the person of St. Peter has received from our Lord Jesus Christ the full power to feed the universal Church, to direct and to guide it, is closely restricted to the exercise of his office as *Pastor* and *Doctor* of all Christians.

The Pope, as visible head of the whole Church, is:

I. The Supreme Teacher of truth revealed by God.

II. The Supreme Priest.

III. The Supreme Legislator in ecclesiastical matters.

IV. The Supreme Judge in ecclesiastical causes.

---

* The Latin of these last words is as follows: 'Doctrinam de fide vel moribus definit;' *i.e.* issues his final decision that a certain doctrine is to be regarded as an essential part of the Catholic faith or of Catholic morality, and to be maintained as such by the universal Church.

The Pope infallible only in his teaching: 43

He has, however, the gift of Infallibility, according to the manifest sense of the words of the definition, only as *supreme teacher of truths necessary for salvation revealed by God*, not as supreme priest, not as supreme legislator in matters of discipline, not as supreme judge in ecclesiastical questions, not in respect of any other questions over which his highest governing power in the Church may otherwise extend.* And when I here decline to place in the range of subjects for the exercise of Infallibility ecclesiastical matters, I mean to exclude all those matters which commonly form the subject of ecclesiastical processes, as, for instance, marriage questions, benefice questions, patronage questions, church-building questions, &c.;

---

* In this sense F. Perrone writes (*Prælect. Theolog.* vol. viii. *De Locis Theologicis*, pars i. § ii. cap. iv. n. 726, Lovanii, 1843, p. 497) : 'Quapropter neque facta personalia, neque præcepta, neque rescripta, neque opiniones, quas identidem promunt Romani Pontifices, neque decreta disciplinæ, neque omissiones definitionis, aliaque id genus plurima in censu veniunt decretorum, de quibus agimus. Quanquam enim hæc omnia pro summâ auctoritate, ex quâ dimanant, magno semper in pretio habenda sint, ac humili mentis obsequio ac veneratione sint excipienda, nihilo tamen minus non constituunt "definitionem ex cathedrâ," de qua loquimur et in quâ solâ adstruimus Pontificiam infallibilitatem.' I quote Perrone as my guarantee, inasmuch as he at least cannot be suspected of wishing to derogate from the Pope's authority. Ballerini expresses himself to the same effect (*De vi ac Ratione Primatûs Rom. Pontif.* cap. xiv. § vi. Veronæ, 1766, p. 287-8) : 'Solas itaque fidei definitiones id (inerrantiæ privilegium) respicit a Summis Pontificibus Ecclesiæ propositas contra insurgentes dissentiones et errores in materiâ fidei : non autem opiniones, quibus etsi aliquid statuant, nihil tamen decernunt credendum ex Catholicâ fide, nihilque damnant tanquam alienum ab eâdem ; non simplicia præcepta, quæ ad fidei definitionem referri non possint ; non judicia de personis tantum, non decreta disciplinæ, quæ ad fidem non pertinent, non tandem omissiones definitionum fidei,' &c.

questions of faith of course the Pope decides as Supreme Teacher.

(2) As doctrinal definitions comprehend doctrines respecting the faith as well as doctrines respecting morals, it will often happen in the nature of things that definitions on the latter of these two subjects, viz. morals, will be issued to the universal Church in the form of a command or prohibition from the Pope (*Precepta morum*).

(3) Here, in order that we may better understand the subject, it will be well to compare what we are now saying with what is said in the third chapter of the Vatican definition *de fide*, where it is expressly taught that the Pope possesses the highest power of jurisdiction over the whole Church, 'not only in matters of faith and morals, but also in matters of the discipline and government of the Church extended over the whole *orbis terrarum*.' ' Non solum in rebus, quæ ad fidem et mores, sed etiam in iis, quæ ad disciplinam et regimen Ecclesiæ per totum orbem diffusæ pertinent.' Thus there are here distinguished four classes of matters as belonging to the province of things ecclesiastical, which fall under the supreme power of the Pope :

I. Matters of faith.
II. Matters of morals.
III. Matters of discipline.
IV. Matters of government.

In all these matters the faithful owe a true obedience to the Pope.

(4) Then in the fourth chapter, entitled 'On the Infallible Teaching Office of the Roman Pope,' the Council treats exclusively of the teaching power of the Pope—matters, that is, of the first and second

class, faith and morals, not matters of the third and fourth class, *i.e.* discipline and government. Accordingly, it is only as regards definitions of the Pope upon faith and morals, that the Council defines, as a proposition revealed by God, that they possess infallible certainty by virtue of the unerring divine assistance promised to the Pope in St. Peter, *i.e.* as the successor of St. Peter. Cardinal Bellarmine had already made this distinction, speaking of the doctrine on morals as follows (*De Rom. Pontif.* lib. iv. cap. v.): 'Non potest errare summus Pontifex in præceptis morum, quæ toti ecclesiæ præscribuntur, et quæ in rebus necessariis ad salutem, vel in iis quæ per se bona et mala sunt, versantur.' What he then says further in this place refers to discipline: 'Non est erroneum dicere Pontificem in aliis legibus posse errare, nimirum superfluam legem condendo vel minus discretam, &c. Ut autem jubeat (sc. Pontifex) aliquid quod non est bonum neque malum ex se, neque contra salutem, sed tamen est inutile, vel sub pœnâ nimis gravi illud præcipiat, non est absurdum dicere posse fieri,' &c. And other theologians follow Bellarmine on this point.

(5) This Infallibility of the Pope in the exercise of his office as Pastor and Doctor of all Christians is, however, still more closely defined as 'that Infallibility with which the Divine Redeemer willed that His Church should be provided in the definition of a doctrine relating to faith or morals.' Before, then, we proceed to answer the question, how far the *Papal* Infallibility extends over matters which concern faith or morals, the question arises how far the Infallibility of the *Church* extends over such matters? Without entering into the investigation of this very wide

question, on which much precise information is afforded in all our great theological works, I content myself with selecting the following proposition, universally acknowledged in theology—viz. 'That even in dogmatic Decrees, Bulls, &c. &c., not all which therein occurs in any one place, not that which occurs or is mentioned incidentally, not a preface, nor what is laid down as the basis of the decree, is to be looked upon as itself a dogmatic definition,* and so as matter of Infallibility.'†

(6) Lastly, the Council adds that the definitions of the Pope, in which, by virtue of his office as Pastor and Doctor, he lays down a certain doctrine on faith or morals as firmly to be held *de fide* by all Christians, are *per se* irreversible, *i.e.* of their own nature, and not only irreversible when they receive the subsequent assent of the Church. It is not meant by this that the Pope ever decides anything contrary to the tradition of the Church, or that he would stand alone in opposition to all the other Bishops, but only that the Infallibility of his definition is not dependent on the acceptance of the Church, and rests on the special divine assistance promised and vouchsafed to him in

---

* If here, as elsewhere, I make use of the term dogmatic definition on a matter of faith in the sense of the Latin words 'dogmatica definitio,' this is only for the sake of brevity. I mean by the words all the 'doctrina de fide et moribus,' following Ballerini (*De vi ac Ratione Primatûs Roman. Pontif.* cap. xv. § v. Veronæ, 1766, p. 312), who thus explains the expression : 'Fidei dogma, in quo continetur et morum naturalis ac divini juris doctrina.'

† 'Quæ in conciliorum vel Pontificum decretis vel explicandi gratiâ inducuntur, vel ut objectioni respondeatur, vel etiam obiter et in transcursu præter institutum præcipuum, de quo erat potissimum controversia, ea non pertinent ad fidem, hoc est, non sunt Catholicæ fidei judicia.'—Melch. Canus, *De Locis Theologicis*, lib. v. cap. v.

the person of St. Peter for the exercise of his supreme teaching office.* Since, then, it is here expressly said that those definitions on which the Infallibility of the Pope exercises itself are *per se* unalterable, it follows, as a matter of course, that all those laws which are issued from time to time by the Pope in matters of discipline, and which *are* alterable, are, by the very reason that they are alterable, not included in the *de fide* definition of the Vatican Council.

10. Having now by these remarks on the *de fide* definitions of the Vatican Council cleared our view of their meaning and import, we find ourselves in a condition to face the conclusions Dr. Schulte draws from them.

The first set of these conclusions may be unhesitatingly admitted—viz. that it is the duty of every Catholic to believe the dogma published on the 18th of July, 1870; that the aim of this solemn proclamation of the doctrine is not merely theoretical but practical—viz. that the Roman Pontiff by these *ex cathedrâ* definitions may make known infallibly those right and true principles of living by which a man must frame his life if he wishes to be happy in the next world; that by this definition not the present Pope alone is declared infallible, but also that each one of his predecessors has been infallible, under those conditions which have been already stated; that such an infallible definition is not conditional on the use of some one or other definite formula; that such a definition is *per se* unalterable, and that its reception by the Church adds nothing to its binding power.

11. Then follows a very important conclusion, commencing with a true proposition, but making, as it is manipulated by Dr. Schulte, a very serious

* See note A, end of this chapter.

divergence from the truth. Dr. Schulte says: 'It is inconceivable that a proposition should be solemnly published as revealed by God, without its also of necessity influencing the faith and life of a Christian.' Again: 'Every man must be able to satisfy himself by objective proofs whether or no such a proposition is really proposed to him.' Again: 'There must be certain objective practical marks whereby every rational being can recognise an utterance *ex cathedrâ*.' Again: 'Those objective proofs must have been always the same, and uninterruptedly.' Again: 'There is an utterance *ex cathedrâ* when the Roman Pontiff utters definitions upon faith and morals which he requires to be looked upon as the teaching of the Church.' This is ascertained, he says, 'sometimes directly from the very words used, sometimes it is gathered from attendant circumstances, sometimes it is evident from the very decision itself, *i.e.* from its subject-matter.' In order, then, to marshal forth these objective practical marks, as he calls them, by which a Papal *ex cathedrâ* utterance may be recognised by any one, he directs his readers' attention to the *objectum*, *i.e.* subject-matter of the infallible teaching office, that is, faith and morals. He then, in the same terms as we do, admits what belongs to faith; but as regards the other subject, morals, he culls from some book of Moral Theology the titles of all the treatises in order to show in detail what belongs to the moral duty of a Christian. Having done this, he proceeds to draw this conclusion: 'Morals comprehend the whole range of the duties in the life of each individual Christian as such.'

This then, being the conclusion drawn by Dr. Schulte, requires of us an exact and careful examination, since in it truth and falsehood are mixed up together in a most dangerous manner, and that which is false serves the writer as a foundation for further misleading developments of his subject.

It is true to say that every truth revealed by God has an influence upon the faith and life of a Christian, and must therefore be capable of being recognised by him in a sure and safe way; and it is true also to say that this character must belong to definitions of the Pope *ex cathedrâ*; and when he asserts that such definitions must be recognisable as such by objective practical marks, this also is, in a certain sense, true. But when he draws his two conclusions— *first*, there is an utterance *ex cathedrâ* whenever the Roman Pontiff utters definitions on faith or morals, and requires that they should be regarded as the teaching of the Church ; and *secondly*, this is made known sometimes directly by the words used, sometimes by attendant circumstances, and sometimes by the very definition itself—then of these two statements of his, the first is true, and the second is false, and the source of many errors.

For it is in this second proposition that Dr. Schulte has set those objective practical marks, as he calls them, whereby a Papal definition has to be recognised as an *ex cathedrâ* utterance. He gives three such objective marks, of which sometimes the first, sometimes the second, sometimes the third, will tell us the will of the Pope as to what we should regard as the teaching of the Church; that is, it is sometimes the words used by the Pope, sometimes the circumstances, sometimes the *very* definition itself; that is, the subject-matter or *objectum* of the definition, his meaning being, when the definition refers to faith or morals in the widest sense of the words.

E

Here, then, it is, in these so-called objective marks, whereby Papal *ex cathedrâ* utterances are supposed to be recognisable, that the dangerous error commences, error which our opponent proceeds to develop further throughout the whole course of his pamphlet.

It will hardly surprise any one who has perused Dr. Schulte's explanatory Preface to his work to be told that Dr. Schulte's very starting-point is unsound and misleading. He assumes, he says, that each individual Catholic Christian must be able, without the intervention of bishop or priest — *i.e.* without having recourse to any teaching authority in the Church—to recognise at once what is an *ex cathedrâ* utterance of the Pope; and this 'because each one has to work out his own salvation.'

Were Dr. Schulte to say that his meaning in these words is (even if he has not said so expressly) that every Catholic can by the assistance of the Church's teaching office (*i.e.* through her bishops and priests) learn what is a Papal utterance *ex cathedrâ*, and therefore infallible, even in the face of conflicting difficulties, then indeed he would explain and rectify his position; but were he to admit this, then indeed he would certainly arrive at a different result from that at which he has actually arrived.

For the bishops and the priests are quite aware that when there is no authentic explanation of a Papal *ex cathedrâ* utterance, the Theological Faculty, which has been for centuries engaged upon this question, has to be heard upon the marks of a real utterance; and that in reality the short *de fide* definition in the Vatican Council in its few words does but contain what the science of Theology has been this long time investigating at great length, with the full knowledge and admission of the difficult questions arising out of the history of ancient times. But we shall look in vain, as Dr. Schulte from his own experience admits, if we wish to find from History or Theology that such Papal utterances are to be recognised, sometimes from the words used, sometimes from the circumstances, and sometimes from the definition itself, as though each one of these marks was of itself sufficient to establish the fact.

On our part, we find that it is the view of Catholic theologians that there are *two* marks of an *ex cathedrâ* utterance, and, moreover, that these two marks must both be found together—viz. that (1) the *objectum* or subject-matter of the decision must be doctrine of faith or morals; and (2) the Pope must express his intention, by virtue of his supreme teaching power, to declare this particular doctrine on faith and morals to be a component part of the truth necessary to salvation revealed by God, and as such to be held by the whole Catholic Church, he must publish it, and so give a formal definition in the matter (*definire*). These two marks must be found together. Any mere circumstances do not suffice to enable a person to recognise what a Pope says as an utterance *ex cathedrâ*, or, in other words, as a *de fide* definition. It is only when the two other marks just mentioned are acknowledged to be present that the circumstances of the case serve to support and strengthen the proof of the Pope's intention; and this intention will be made known by his own words.

Should, however, these marks not give us a certainty absolutely free from all doubt as to whether, in a certain case, there is a Papal utterance *ex* *cathedrâ*, then will the subordinate teaching authority of the Church have recourse to the highest Authority himself, to ask him what his intention was in such an utterance,* or to ask whether a former Papal utterance on such and such a matter is to be looked upon as *ex cathedrâ*.

Here it must be evident to every one that from this point Dr. Schulte's way of viewing his subject and my own must part company in their further development, viz. as to what is and is not an infallible doctrine uttered by the Pope.

He lays down three notes, of which three any one alone is enough to make known a Papal utterance as infallible, and therefore unalterable, as being *ex cathedrâ*.

I, on the contrary, having regard to the words and the import of the definition of the Vatican Council, and also bearing in mind previous scientific expositions of theologians on the subject, lay down two such notes, both of which, however, must always be found together; whilst to the third note I attribute only an auxiliary significance.

As was to be expected, Dr. Schulte, in consequence, naturally finds a great number of Papal *ex*

* Such an appeal to the Pope is not, then, so absurd as Dr. Schulte says; on the contrary, where there is a supreme authority, it is quite intelligible and reasonable on the part of the Pope's subordinates in matters on which a doubt might arise of the applicability of the Pope's intention to a particular case, although in the first instance the intention was clearly expressed.

(Of course Bishop Fessler is here understood as meaning that this fresh explanation of the definition must be provided with all the marks which are necessary to prove the presence of a real definition; just as in a will any alteration or explanation forming part of a will, must be attested by the same witnesses and with the same formalities as were required for the original document. TRANSLATOR.)

cathedrâ utterances; I, in accordance with the Theological Faculty, find only a few.

12. Having made his own exposition of notes of a definition, Dr. Schulte proceeds to assert 'that only the Pope himself can define the subject-matter, the comprehensiveness, and the limits of an utterance *ex cathedrâ.*' This assertion is so far true, that it is certain that no human authority can prescribe anything to the Pope in this matter. If, however, it is meant that the Pope, according to his own will and fancy, can at all events extend his infallible definition even to matters relating to the *Jus publicum*, to which the divine revelation does not extend, then he has laid the case before us quite erroneously. The Pope, in his doctrinal utterances, only speaks what he finds, under the special divine assistance, to be already part of the truth revealed by God necessary for salvation, which He has given in trust to the Catholic Church (*i.e.* in the divine *depositum fidei*). The same assistance of God which securely preserves the Pope from error preserves him with equal security from declaring *that* to be revealed by God, and intrusted to the keeping of the Catholic Church as a matter of truth or morals, which God has *not* revealed and has *not* deposited in His Church.*

Supposing then, as Dr. Schulte says, 'the infallible teaching office of the Church can even extend to all subjects and departments of man's life which have any bearing upon his moral conduct,' yet assuredly no infallible doctrine will ever be pronounced which is not part of the truth revealed by God. Were the contrary of this possible, then would God have for-

* See note B of the editor of the French translation at the end of this chapter.

saken His Church, which is impossible, since we have His promise that He will never forsake her unto the end of the world; and to this promise we both *are* and *must* continue faithful if we desire to be Catholics and to remain so.

13. Dr. Schulte now passes on to the special practical matter of his pamphlet, and says: 'In order, then, to proceed to investigate with certainty what is the doctrine of the Church in respect to the relations between the spiritual and temporal power, we must have recourse to the utterances of the Pope. What these utterances have declared as really proceeding from him, *that* is the truth, and *that* must be believed by every Catholic, and must be the rule of his conduct.'

Hereupon Dr. Schulte proceeds to represent in the following manner what the doctrine of the Church is in respect of the relations of the spiritual to the temporal power, which the Catholic Christian must believe and follow out, if the infallible teaching office of the Pope is a matter of faith.* Well, he may do so. But it must be our business to insist upon this—viz. that in his representation he shall only represent *that* to be matter of faith which is really and truly a definition of the Pope on faith and morals. If he does not do this—if he represents Papal rescripts which belong to the province of reversible legislation, or are mere acts of government, as definitions of Popes upon faith and morals, or if from the records of real dogmatic defini-

---

* In the Introduction, p. 18 of his Pamphlet, he thus expresses his own intention: 'I, in the first instance, issue this pamphlet that governments and persons governed may be thoroughly acquainted with what a Catholic who admits the Infallibility of the Pope is bound to believe as matter of conscience.'

tions of Popes he extracts mere incidental remarks, *obiter dicta*, and alleges these to be *ex cathedrâ*—then assuredly he is leading his readers into error; he is disturbing their consciences without reason; he is arousing the suspicions of governments unnecessarily, and setting them against that Catholic doctrine which has been declared by the Vatican Council; and he is consciously or unconsciously (God only knows which) creating great prejudice against the Catholic Church.

Dr. Schulte is unfortunate with his proofs from the very commencement. For instance, in order to prove that 'what the Popes have declared to be a doctrine of the Church is true, and to be believed by all Catholics, and followed by them in practice,'* he, without further introduction, brings the following

* I said designedly above, p. 44, 'only a real and true definition of the Pope on faith and morals' can be under consideration, because the expression made use of by Dr. Schulte, p. 27 of his Pamphlet, is ambiguous. He says : 'What the Popes have declared to be such' (viz. a dogma of the Church), 'that is true, and must be believed by Catholics, and accordingly followed by them in practice.' This may be true and may be false. For not all that the Popes have declared to be a doctrine of the Church is for that reason alone (because the Popes have said so) true, and to be believed by Catholics, and so followed by them in practice; but only that which Popes have declared in an *ex cathedrâ* utterance to be a dogma of faith or morals to be believed by the whole Church. See Ballerini, l. c. p. 36, who speaks very expressly on this point: 'Multæ sententiæ, quæ in Pontificum sive epistolis, sive concionibus, sive aliis quibuslibet eorum operibus inspersæ, etiam si veritatem aut aliquod dogma contineant, et verissimæ sint, non tamen fidei definitiones dici queunt, sicuti similes sententiæ in aliis Patribus inventæ, opinionis vel dogmatis, uti materies fert, testimonia sunt, definitiones autem fidei non item.' So also says Cardinal Bellarmine: 'Multa esse in epistolis decretalibus, quæ non faciunt, rem aliquam esse de fide, sed solum opiniones Pontificum ea in re nobis declarant.' *De Rom. Pontif.* lib. iv. c. xiv.

proof. 'For,' says he, 'Pope Leo X. asserts in his Bull *Exurge Domine* of June 15, 1520, which excommunicates Luther and rejects his teaching, §. 6, "Had Luther done this" (viz. come to Rome), " we should have proved to him, as clear as the light of day, that the holy Roman Popes our predecessors have never erred in their canons or constitutions."' And this is an *ex cathedrâ* utterance! Dr. Schulte really means it, for he adds in a note, 'Can any one venture to say that the words we have just quoted are not an *ex cathedrâ* utterance?' Had he quoted the passage in full from which he clips this morsel, and presented it to his readers, any candid reader would have been able to judge whether such a cursory remark could, by any possibility, be erected into a dogma of the faith, *i.e.* a real *ex cathedrâ* Papal utterance. So I will bring forward the whole passage, that the reader may judge for himself. It runs as follows: ' Had he, Martin Luther, done this' (viz., as the context shows, 'had Luther come to Rome'), 'then would he assuredly, *as we think*, have entered into himself and acknowledged his errors; nor would he have found so many faults in the Roman Curia, which he so violently attacks, giving an undue weight to the empty words of mischievous persons; and we should have shown him clearer than the light of day that the holy Roman Popes our predecessors, whom he traduces in such unmeasured terms, have never erred in those canons and constitutions of theirs, which he studiously assails.'*

* ' Quod si fecisset pro certo, ut arbitramur, ad cor reversus errores suos cognovisset nec in Romanâ curiâ quam tantopere vanis malevolorum rumoribus plus quam oportuit tribuendo, vituperat, tot reperiisset errata ; docuissemusque eum clarius luce

Are we bound to look upon the particular parts of this passage as Papal utterances *ex cathedrâ*, even when the Pope says himself 'as we think' (*ut arbitramur*)? Or how can Dr. Schulte possibly claim for himself the right out of three principal propositions, apart from dependent propositions, to dock off the first and second propositions as not dogmatic,* and to bring forward the third clause, and that not entire, and allege this to be an infallible utterance? If Dr. Schulte assigns as his reason for taking out of the context this third proposition, and bringing it forward as an infallible utterance, because the Pope here says that if Luther had come to Rome, he, the Pope, would have taught him that the Popes have never erred in their canons or constitutions, and that he selects this passage as an instance of his infallible teaching, because the Pope speaks expressly of *teaching* Luther, then I answer, not everything which the Popes *might have* taught, but what they actually *have* taught as doctrine on faith and morals, and defined,† by virtue of their highest apostolical power, as true, and to be held as such by the universal Church, *that* alone is an infallible utterance *ex cathedrâ*. Perhaps Dr. Schulte may here say, 'You may see plainly enough from the words of Pope Leo X. what his thoughts were, and *how* he hoped to teach Luther if

---

sanctos Romanos Pontifices predecessores nostros, quos præter omnem modestiam injuriose lacerat, in suis canonibus seu constitutionibus, quas mordere nititur, nunquam errasse. *Bullarium Romanum*, ed. Cocquelines, tom. iii. p. iii. Romæ, 1743, p. 491.

* For Dr. Schulte has omitted after the word 'constitutions' the words which in the Papal bull immediately follow, viz. ' which he studiously assails ;' words which contain a limitation of the foregoing general expression, 'constitutiones.'

† 'Definit' is the well-considered word of the Vatican Council.

he actually had gone to Rome.' To this I answer, 'It is quite beside the moot question what a Pope's *thoughts* were; nor does it at all belong to a Papal utterance *ex cathedrâ* to consider what a Pope *thinks*, or even what a Pope thinks it well to give as a piece of private advice or *information* to any one in this or that manner.'

After this first most unfortunate proof which Dr. Schulte has brought forward, he tries a second, which is not a bit better. Accordingly he says: 'Just so has it been declared in express words by Pius IX. on the occasion of the condemnation of a book: "Finally, not to mention other errors, he rises to such a pitch of audacity and impiety* as with indescribable perversion to assert "that the Roman Pontiffs and Ecumenical Councils have overstepped the limits of their power, assumed for themselves the rights of princes, and have even erred in matters of faith and morals.'"† Here I should like to ask, in sober earnest, whether any one ever before Dr. Schulte took it into his head to assert that dogmatic infallible definitions (utterances *ex cathedrâ*) were sent forth by Popes as mere accessory matter on the occasion of the condemnation of a book? There is nothing whatever in all the fundamental principles of the theological science which can be brought forward to prove this, and

---

* The German word 'Gottlosigkeit,' which is rendered above by 'impiety,' is an imperfect translation of the Latin 'impietas' (so also is our English word 'impiety.'—Tr.). The words 'pius,' 'impius,' 'pietas,' and 'impietas,' all designate a certain state of mind towards God as well as a state of mind towards parents, and 'impietas' is here used in this latter sense, inasmuch as the Pope is regarded as the 'pastor omnium Christianorum' in the sentence quoted from the Brief in question.

† See Brief *Multiplices inter*, June 10, 1851.

therefore it is a purely gratuitous assertion that a Papal document by which a bad book is rejected and forbidden (the reasons being assigned) is on that account raised to the rank of a dogmatic definition, and the reasons assigned by the Pope for the condemnation of a book stamped as Papal utterances *ex cathedrâ.**

The third and last proof of an infallible utterance which Dr. Schulte brings forward is closely connected with the second; it runs : ' And resting on this Brief, the Syllabus, in no. xxiii., condemns the proposition— " Roman Pontiffs and Ecumenical Councils have transgressed the limits of their power, have claimed for themselves the rights of princes, and have erred

* In a note to page 28 of his pamphlet he assumes as proved that this Brief speaks *ex cathedrâ*, and this he does for the following reasons : 1. 'It appeals to the duty of preserving the flock of Christ, which has been committed to him (the Pope) from the first Pastor.' Here I ask, to preserve from what ? Dr. Schulte prudently holds his tongue upon this point, since it makes nothing for his point. But the context says plainly what this is. 'It is to preserve men from the pernicious reading bad books, and keeping them in their possession.' That is expressly declared by the Pope to be the object of this Brief, not a definition on a matter of faith. The further reasons he gives are not a whit more to the purpose; as, 2. 'The Pope speaks of his apostolical office.' 3. 'Of his apostolical plenitude of power.' As if he didn't do this every time he exercised his supreme power in the Church. 4. 'The Pope commands open publication.' As if nothing was ever published openly except definitions on matters of faith, and as if prohibited books were not so published. 5. ' He refers therein to the Syllabus.' Just as if all that the Syllabus refers to is, for that very reason, *i.e.* because it is in the Syllabus, at once to be looked on as a dogmatic definition on a matter of faith. 6. 'He decides after a mature consideration, with the advice of the cardinals.' Just as if many other things were not decided after mature consideration, and with the advice of the cardinals. If the circumstances which Dr. Schulte speaks of as proofs of what is *ex cathedrâ* are something of this sort, it is easy to see how utterly valueless such ' circumstances' are, to enable him to make out his point.

in their decisions upon faith and morals."' Thus, amongst the doctrines of the Church he conclusively places the following proposition: 'Roman Popes have not overstepped the limits of their power, have not usurped the rights of princes, have not erred in their declarations on faith and morals.' In bringing forward this passage from the Syllabus, Dr. Schulte has not definitely asserted that he looks upon it as a dogmatic definition—a Papal utterance, that is, *ex cathedrâ*. As he has not done this, he has saved me the trouble of going farther into the matter. It is sufficient for us to direct attention to the fact, that when in the first and second parts of this proposition of the Syllabus, it is said that the Roman Pontiffs have, *first*, 'not overstepped the limits of their power,' and, *secondly*, that they 'have not usurped the rights of princes,' these assertions have no reference to a truth revealed by God, but bear upon historical events of a later period, which events have nothing to do with faith and morals, but only with the acts of the Popes. So it is plain there is not here the *objectum* or subject-matter required for a dogmatic definition.

Our readers can now judge for themselves that these three proofs of infallible teaching which Dr. Schulte has confidently brought forward (and he only brings forward these three) are anything but valid or perfect proofs of his assertion, that Popes, in their infallible definitions, or utterances *ex cathedrâ*, have set forth as the doctrine of the Church, or *de fide*, these propositions: 1st, that Popes have never erred in their constitutions; 2d, that they have never overstepped the limits of their power; or, 3d, claimed for themselves the rights of princes. If Dr. Schulte has not proved this, as he most certainly has not, then his assertion falls to the ground, 'that a Catholic, in accepting the *de fide* definition of the Vatican Council " on the Infallible teaching office of the Roman Pontiff," is bound to believe that the Popes have *never* erred in their constitutions; that they have *never* overstepped the limits of their power; have *never* claimed for themselves the rights of princes.' Here, however, I must take care not to be misunderstood. I say only that a man is not bound by a definition *de fide* of the Vatican Council to believe all this besides; which is what Dr. Schulte, on untenable grounds, imagines that he discovers to be contained in this particular *de fide* definition.*

Such is the poor outcome of the fundamental proposition on which Dr. Schulte has erected his whole edifice in this Pamphlet.

* What should be the way in which a Catholic should conduct himself as regards these propositions of the Papal Brief, *Multiplices inter*, June 10, 1851, and also as regards the Syllabus, no. xxiii. (even if they are not doctrinal definitions), see above, 9 (3), and compare Ballerini, *De vi ac Ratione Primatûs Romanorum Pontificum*, Veronæ, 1766, cap. xv. § 10.

Note A to No. 9 (6), chap. ii. p. 37.

M. Emmanuel Cosquin, the Editor of the French translation of Bishop Fessler's Pamphlet, has appended the following note to page 37, for the accuracy of which he makes himself responsible. He says:

'In order to complete what Mgr. Fessler here says, we borrow a passage from the *Pastoral Instruction* of the Swiss Bishops in June 1871, which has been approved by a Brief of Pius IX. "The Definition of the Council," say the Swiss Bishops, "has not in any respect brought about a separation between the head and the members of the teaching body in the Church. After the Council, as before, the Popes will exercise their office as Doctors and Chief Pastors in the Church, without forgetting that the Bishops are appointed with them by the Holy Spirit, and, according to the constitution of the Church, as successors of the Apostles, in order that, in concert with the Pope and in subordination to the successor of the Prince of the Apostles, they may govern the Church of God. As the Popes did before the Council, so now after it will they continue to strengthen their brethren the Bishops in the Faith; so also, in the government of the Church, never will they undertake anything which concerns the Universal Church without taking the counsel and advice of the Bishops. As they did before the Council, so now also afterwards, will the Popes summon Councils; ask the advice of the Bishops scattered over the world; use every means in their power to obtain a full understanding respecting that deposit of the Faith which has been confided to the Church. It will be according to this only and immutable rule of the Faith that they will decide, as if in court of supreme and last instance, and infallibly, for the Universal Church, all questions which can possibly arise on matters of Faith or Morals.

"Nevertheless," add the Swiss Bishops, "even when the Popes use all possible means to obtain a profound knowledge of the question of the Faith which is under consideration, as the duties of their office require, yet is it not this purely human knowledge, however complete it may be, but it is the assistance of the Holy Spirit—that is to say, it is a special grace of his state peculiar to himself—which gives the Pope the indubitable assurance of Infallibility, and which guarantees to all the faithful, with an absolute certainty, that the definitions of faith of the supreme teaching authority of the Pope are exempt from error." '

Note B to No. 12, chap. ii. p. 43.

The French Editor has here another important note:

' In their *Pastoral Instruction*, posterior to the work of Mgr. Fessler, and approved, as is known, by Pius IX., the Swiss Bishops cite the following passage of the Constitution of the Vatican Council : " The Holy Spirit has not been promised to the successors of St. Peter that they might publish according to His revelations a new doctrine, but in order that with His assistance they may holily guard and faithfully set forth the revelation transmitted by the Apostles—that is to say, the deposit of the Faith." And they add : " It is, then, the revelation given by God, the deposit of the Faith, which is the domain perfectly traced out and exactly circumscribed, within which the infallible decisions of the Pope are able to extend themselves, and in regard to which the faith of Catholics can be bound to fresh obligations. . . . It in no way depends upon the caprice of the Pope, or upon his good pleasure, to make such and such a doctrine the object of a dogmatic definition : he is tied up and limited to the divine revelation, and to the truths which that revelation contains; he is tied up and limited by the Creeds already in existence, and by the preceding definitions of the Church ; he is tied up and limited by the divine law, and by the constitution of the Church; lastly, he is tied up and limited by that doctrine, divinely revealed, which affirms that alongside religious society there is civil society; that alongside the Ecclesiastical Hierarchy there is the power of Temporal Magistrates, invested in their own domain with a full sovereignty, and to whom we owe in conscience obedience and respect in all things morally permitted, and which belong to the domain of civil society." '

CHAPTER III.

'DOCTRINAL PROPOSITIONS OF THE POPE, SIMPLE AND "EX CATHEDRA."—ACTS OF POPES BEARING UPON THEIR RELATIONS TOWARDS STATES, COUNTRIES, PEOPLES, AND INDIVIDUALS.'

14. IN this portion of his treatise, Dr. Schulte has been at the utmost pains to rake together from every quarter, especially from the middle ages, everything odious he can find against the Popes.

In order to throw light upon this chapter of his Pamphlet, I must call the attention of my reader to the results of the investigation I made in the preceding chapter on the true extent of the subject-matter of Papal Infallibility according to the *de fide* definition of the Vatican Council, as a right appreciation of what follows depends strictly on what I have already said.

(1.) Thus, in my present answer I have nothing to do with what the Popes have thought, or said, or done, or ordained to be done, but only with what they have defined to be a doctrine of faith or morals *ex cathedrâ*, and the propositions on the faith which a Catholic must therefore accept as already decided in *ex cathedrâ* utterances by the Popes, in virtue of their Infallible supreme teaching authority, if, as he is in duty bound to do, he accepts the *de fide* definition of the Vatican Council.

(2.) Acts of Popes undoubtedly are not Papal utterances *ex cathedrâ*.

(3.) All that Popes have said in daily life, or in

books of which they are the authors (supposing them, *i.e.*, to have written books), or in ordinary letters, are not dogmatic definitions or utterances *ex cathedrâ*.

(4.) Utterances of Popes, either to individuals or to the whole Church, even in their solemn rescripts, made by virtue of their supreme power of jurisdiction, in issuing disciplinary laws, in judicial decrees* and penal enactments, and in other acts of ecclesiastical government, are not dogmatic Papal definitions or infallible utterances *ex cathedrâ*.

(5.) Accordingly, none of these matters, acts of Popes (2), what Popes have said (3), utterances of Popes (4), have anything to do with the subject we have under discussion—which is exclusively about Infallible definitions.

(6.) Moreover, if we have before us a real and true dogmatic definition of the Pope, still only that portion of it is to be looked upon and accepted as an *ex cathedrâ* utterance, which is expressly designated as 'the Definition;' and nothing whatever is to be so regarded which is only mentioned as accessory matter.

Now, then, having laid down these general rules for our guidance, when I come to examine this portion of Dr. Schulte's treatise, I have to keep the two following questions, which arise out of it, entirely separate, and to give them a separate answer. They are:

First, whether the particular propositions, which he arrays for our consideration, have been defined by an infallible Papal utterance as Catholic doctrine *de fide* on faith or morals?

---

* See no. 9 (1), (3), and (4), for an explanation of these two terms.

And, secondly, if they are not this, then what is really to be held as regards these propositions?

15. So, in considering these propositions, I shall begin by answering the first of these questions, which it is clear, from the object Dr. Schulte has in view in his Pamphlet, is the principal question.

The FIRST Proposition which he brings before us as Papal doctrine is: 'Temporal power is of the Evil One, and must therefore be subject to the Pope.'

For this proposition he refers to a certain Brief of Gregory VII. where, however, it is not found in these express words, and where the context gives a different meaning. But Dr. Schulte himself adds, 'These passages, however, are not uttered *ex cathedrâ.*' As he says this himself, he saves me the trouble of proving that his proposition has nothing to do with Papal Infallibility, and cannot therefore be here considered.

16. The SECOND Proposition is: 'The temporal power must always act unconditionally in subordination to the directions of the spiritual.'

In proof that this proposition is a Papal utterance *ex cathedrâ*, Dr. Schulte brings forward the celebrated Bull *Unam Sanctam* of Pope Boniface VIII. This Bull, starting with a *de fide* proposition of the Nicene-Constantinopolitan Creed, which has so long existed in the Church, contains a detailed exposition of the mutual relations of the temporal and the spiritual power; and ends with a dogmatic definition, which is as follows: 'And this we declare, we say, we define, and we pronounce, that it is necessary for the salvation of every human creature that he should be subject to the Roman Pontiff.'* These words, and only these words, are the definition *de fide* of the Bull *Unam Sanctam*. All the rest of the foregoing, after the very first words, which lay down an acknowledged article of faith as a basis, is a partly theological, partly canonical exposition of the relative positions of Church and State, made after the fashion of viewing such matters then in vogue; but it constitutes no dogmatic definition at all, which evidently commences with the words, 'We declare and we define (*definimus*).'† The definition itself asserts only the Catholic doctrine of the *Primacy* of the Roman Pontiff;‡ for if the Pope has been appointed by

* 'Porro subesse Romano Pontifici omni creaturæ humanæ declaramus, dicimus, definimus, et pronunciamus, omnino esse de necessitate salutis.' *Extravag. Commun.* c. i. De Majorit. et Obed. The expression 'omni humanæ creaturæ' is borrowed from the First Catholic Epistle of St. Peter, c. ii. v. 13, and in the Fifth Lateran Council it is explained by Pope Leo X. as meaning 'omnes Christi fideles' (Harduin's *Acta Concil.* tom. ix. Paris, 1714, col. 1830). I have further to remark, that the Latin word of the above definition, '*subesse*,' is correctly and exactly expressed by the word 'unterstehen,' Ang. 'to stand under.'

† If Pope Boniface VIII. had wished to declare all that is represented in the Bull respecting the relations of the temporal to the spiritual power to be a definition *de fide*, he need only have placed the word 'definimus,' 'we define,' at its commencement. But this he did not do; and if a man who, amongst all the Popes, is distinguished by his ability as a legislator, places the decisive word, not at the *commencement* of the whole Decretal, but before the *concluding* words, as we have just accurately stated, surely no one can be entitled to assert that all that precedes these words is a Papal doctrinal definition.

‡ That is, the *spiritual*, to the omission from the definition of any mention of the *temporal* power. This is clearly proved from the fact that the words of Boniface, 'Subesse Romano Pontifici esse de necessitate salutis,' are taken from St. Thomas, *Opusc. I., contr. Error. Græc.* c. 32: 'Ostenditur etiam, quod subesse Romano Pontifici sit de necessitate salutis. . . . Maximus in Epistolâ orientali-

God to be the Head of His Church, and if every one who cares for the good of his soul must belong to that Church, then it follows that he must be subordinate to the Pope as the Head of the Church (*subesse Romano Pontifici*). This surely is a truth which Catholic princes have ever acknowledged, and I do not imagine any Catholic prince denies it at the present day.

It will be said, no doubt, 'Yes, in spiritual things the Catholic prince is subject to the Pope, but not in temporal things.' To this I answer: The decision of the above-named decretal contains nothing whatever about the Catholic prince being under the Pope in temporal things; still less does it say, as Dr. Schulte formulates his second proposition, 'That the temporal power must act unconditionally in subordination to the spiritual.'

But here again, perhaps, I shall be answered, 'True, it is not said so, but it is implied.'

To this I answer: According to the exposition, partly theological, partly canonical, certainly it might be supposed that this was the meaning; but it is a general rule that whenever, in any dogmatic definition, a question to which it gives rise has not been touched upon (as is here the case with the question whether this definition extends to temporal matters), then this question is to be looked upon as still undefined.* It

bus directâ dicit : " Coadunatam et fundatam super petram confessionis Petri dicimus universalem Ecclesiam secundum definitionem Salvatoris, in qua necessario salutis animarum nostrarum est remanere et ei est obedire, suam servantes fidem et confessionem." '
TRANSLATOR.

* Here we have just such a case as Perrone expressly speaks of above, at p. 43, calling it *omissio definitionis*, which he says cannot constitute an *ex cathedrâ* utterance ; thus the positive extent (*tragweite*) of a definition is to be measured, not by what is *left unsaid*, but by what *is said*.

equally a definition de fide.

would have been defined if the Pope had said in his definition 'that every human being was subject to the Pope, not only in spiritual but also in temporal matters.' But then the Pope did not say this, although the question lay, so to speak, at his elbow.

It may be still further objected: 'Well, if the Pope did not *say* so, he has shown clearly enough the plain common sense and import of the definition by his conduct towards King Philip resulting directly from this Bull.'

I answer again: Granting even the intention of the Pope in this definition did go beyond the plain words, and indeed so far beyond them as the subsequent conduct of Pope Boniface VIII. towards King Philip indicates, still we must not overlook the fact that a mere intention, even if it may be assumed from actions to have existed, if it is not expressed (especially when it might easily have been expressed), is not to be looked upon as a dogmatic definition. Moreover, it must not be forgotten that Pope Clement V., in an explanation which he afterwards made on the extension of this definition, recalled the legitimate interpretation of the Bull to its right proportions;* and this interpretation probably corresponded with the real intention of Pope Boniface VIII. as far as can be gathered from his acts.†

For the rest it may be conceded that in this constitution *Unam Sanctam* of Pope Boniface VIII. there

* Vide *Extravag. Com.* c. ii. *Meruit: De Privilegiis.*

† It is therefore carefully to be noted, as a matter of great importance, that the renewal and approbation of the constitution of Boniface VIII.'s Bull *Unam Sanctam*, at the eleventh session of the Fifth Lateran Council (see Harduin, *Acta Concil.* tom. ix. Paris, 1714, col. 1830), took place only after the addition of the declaration of Pope Clement V. contained in the afore-named decretal, *Meruit*.

is a second dogmatic definition, and it is this: 'That there are not, according to the vain fancy and erroneous teaching of the Manichees, two principles.'* This is *de fide*, since in theology it serves as a sure note of a dogmatic definition when an opposite doctrine is branded by the Pope as heretical, as is the case here, where the doctrine at variance with the true doctrine is stigmatised as 'heretical.'

17. The THIRD Proposition of Dr. Schulte is: 'The Church is entitled to bestow and to take away every temporal sovereignty.'

(1.) His first proof is taken from the words of Pope Gregory VII. spoken in a solemn session of a Council at Rome in the year 1080. Well, what *are* the words which Dr. Schulte brings forward? Our readers will be astonished to hear. They are a prayer which the Pope addresses to the two Apostles, St. Peter and St. Paul, earnestly entreating them to exercise the just judgment, which God has committed to them, on the Emperor Henry IV., and so to make manifest that in very deed they can both take away and can bestow upon this earth empires, kingdoms, principalities, and the possessions of all men, according to the deserts of the individual. And this prayer to the Apostles, forsooth, is to be construed into a dogmatic definition? To expect that his readers will admit that, is assuredly to suppose them to be very deficient in judgment.

(2.) He continues: 'It is a fact that Gregory VII. did depose King Henry IV., did release his subjects from their oath of allegiance, and did install Rudolph

---

* 'Nisi duo (sicut Manichæus) fingat esse principia, quod falsum et hæreticum judicamus.'

in his place.' Well, that is an action of the Pope,* but it is not an Infallible definition which a Catholic must accept.

(3.) Again: 'Pope Gregory IX., in the year 1239, declares the Emperor Frederick II. excommunicated, and releases from their oath of allegiance† all who had pledged their fidelity to him.' Well, that is a penal sentence whereby excommunication, with all its legitimate consequences according to the laws of that period, was fulminated on the offender; but it is not a definition of faith, it is not an utterance of the Pope *ex cathedrâ* upon faith or morals at all, as anybody who will open his eyes may see.

(4.) The same answer holds good in regard to the deposition of the above-named Emperor Frederick II. by Innocent IV. in the year 1245, in which were bound up the consequences of such a sentence, accord-

* As regards both this and the following points, I must again call my reader's attention to the fact that, for greater clearness, I keep the two questions quite separate in my explanation, viz. first, whether the acts and expressions of the Popes brought under our notice in Dr. Schulte's propositions are definitions made by the Pope in his Infallible teaching office, and therefore to be regarded, according to the Vatican Council, as Catholic doctrine *de fide*; and, secondly, if this is not the case, then 'what is to be thought of these acts and expressions?' Strictly speaking, the first question alone belongs to the object of this reply of mine to Dr. Schulte; and if I can prove that nothing that he brings forward belongs to Papal Infallibility in the sense of the Vatican Council, then Dr. Schulte's Pamphlet is sufficiently answered. But for the sake of my readers who may perhaps be disquieted on account of these acts and expressions of Popes which Dr. Schulte brings into notice, though they do not really belong at all to the Infallible teaching office, and are not subject-matter for the faith of a Catholic, I will not fail to direct their attention to the leading points of view in order to guide them to a right judgment on these subjects.

† So in the Bull *Quia Fridericus*, in the *Bullar. Rom.*, ed. cit. t. iii. p. 292.

ing to what was the *Jus publicum* common in those times.*

(5.) 'Pope Nicholas V. deposed the Antipope Felix, (Duke Amadeus of Savoy) in the year 1447, and declared all his possessions confiscated, as the possessions of an anathematised heretic.'† Neither is this a definition of faith, but an execution of the punishment which, according to the *Jus publicum* common in those times, was bound up with the Anathema, an execution (*executio*) with which, in this case, the King of France was charged.‡

(6.) No more is there a dogmatic definition before us in the Papal Bull whereby King Henry VIII. of England, in the year 1535, was threatened with an excommunication, carried into effect in the year 1538, with all its legal consequences, according to the *Jus publicum* common in those times.§ It is a simple penal sentence in the spirit and in the form which once was customary, but which in later times fell into disuse.

(7.) The same holds good of the penal sentence pronounced upon Queen Elizabeth of England by Pope Pius V., issued in the year 1570.||

* So in the Bull *Ad Apostolicæ*, in the *Bullar. Rom.*, edit. cit. t. iii. p. 300, and in the Acts of the Council of Lyons, I. Session iii.; Harduin's *Acta Concil.* t. vii. Paris, 1714, col. 381.

† Raynaldi, *Annal. Eccles.*, ad ann. 1447, n. 18 (t. xviii. p. 338), and compare this with ad ann. 1446, n. 11 (ibid. p. 325).

‡ 'Brachium auxilii sæcularis Caroli regis Francorum invocandi facultatem concedimus,' says the Pope to the Archbishop of Aix, to whom this despatch is addressed.

§ In the Bull *Ejus qui*, in the *Bullar. Rom.*, edit. cit. t. iv. p. i. p. 125, and so in the Bull *Cum Redemptor*, in the *Bullar. Rom.*, l. c. p. 130.

|| In the Bull *Regnans in Excelsis*, in the *Bullar. Rom.*, ed. cit. t. iv. p. iii. p. 98.

Now, since all the Bulls here brought forward— (3) to (7)—have not the faintest trace of being Papal, doctrinal, or *de fide* definitions, utterances of the Popes *ex cathedrâ*; and since they plainly and uncontestably belong to an entirely different class of Papal deliveries, it clearly follows that no one of these is to be regarded as an infallible utterance of Popes, and this alone it is which, by the definition of the Vatican Council, a Catholic is to believe and obey as part of the doctrine of the Catholic Church. It is hardly credible that a learned man like Dr. Schulte should have asserted all these Bulls to be infallible. Such an assertion is both unscientific and contrary to common sense. If, however, he has not put forward this assertion in earnest, why has he piled up all these quotations out of the Bulls he has ransacked, which have really nothing whatever to do with the teaching office of the Pope?

(8.) Dr. Schulte proceeds with another Bull of Pope Paul IV., issued in the year 1559,* which is rightly described in the collection of Papal Bulls under the title of 'Renewal of previous censures and punishments against heretics and schismatics, with the addition of further penalties.' Why, the very title, which gives a true account of its contents, is of itself alone enough to show every one who reads it, that this Papal delivery is not a definition *de fide*, and cannot, therefore, be an utterance *ex cathedrâ*. And yet Dr. Schulte, in the most decided way, asserts that it is, saying that 'it is directed to the whole Church, signed by the Cardinals in the most solemn form,

* *Vide* the Bull *Cum ex Apostolatus*, in the *Bullar. Rom.*, ed. cit. t. iv. p. i. p. 354. 'Innovatio quarumcumque censurarum et pœnarum contra hæreticos et schismaticos,' &c.

so that it is certainly delivered *ex cathedrâ*' (Dr. Schulte's Pamphlet, p. 34).* One can hardly believe one's eyes when one sees such manifestly erroneous assertions set forth with such an affectation of demonstrated certainty. One really feels sorry for Dr. Schulte that he should have made such an enormous blunder in the sight of every one who knows anything at all about such matters. To us it is beyond all question certain, that this Bull is not a definition of faith or morals, not an utterance *ex cathedrâ*. It is simply an outcome of the supreme Papal authority as legislator, and an instance of his exercising his power of punishing; it is not done in the exercise of his power as supreme teacher. I should abuse the patience of my readers if I were to attempt to prove in detail what is manifest to all mankind in every line of the Bull. Who ever imagined before Dr. Schulte that the Pope was infallible in the province of declaring legal pains and penalties?

Dr. Schulte finds in this Bull various things which he designates by the terms 'remarkable!' 'still more remarkable!' 'most remarkable!' until he comes to the epithet 'inconceivable!' pp. 34, 35. And indeed it is 'very remarkable,' nay quite 'inconceivable,' that Dr. Schulte, who is a canonist, should have so utterly misunderstood the introduction to this Bull, and the sense of a passage further on in it, § 6. I am conscious I am giving utterance to a grave reproof, and I must entreat my reader's patience while I prove it. Dr. Schulte finds it 'very remarkable;'

---

* It must seem quite ridiculous to any one who has any sort of knowledge of the subject to hear a person boldly assert that such and such a Papal Bull must be infallible, because it is directed to the whole Church and signed by all the Cardinals.

he says that 'the election of a heretic as Pope is valueless from the first, and is here declared to be null and void.' That is, he says, 'The Pope and Cardinals assume the possibility of an infallible Pope being found deviating from the faith!'

To set this supposed case in its proper light the following remarks may be useful. Pope Paul IV., no doubt, supposes the case possible (however improbable it might be) that a man who clings to an heretical doctrine might be chosen Pope, and also that after he has mounted the Papal throne, he might still hold heretical doctrine, or, even it may be, express it in his intercourse with others; not, however, that he would teach the whole Church this heretical doctrine in an utterance of his supreme teaching office (*ex cathedrâ*). From making such an utterance God Himself, through His special assistance, preserves the Pope and the Church. If, then, as has been suggested, a man were elected Pope who might uphold heretical doctrine (not supposing that he could declare such a doctrine to the whole Church formally as Catholic doctrine *de fide*, or prescribe it to be held as such), then we should have the case before us for which Pope Paul IV., in the above-named Bull, § 6, provides, by quashing the election of such a man to the Papacy, and declaring it 'null and void.' This is one of the cases which theologians mean when they say the Pope (*homo privatus*), as a private individual, may err in a matter of faith; that is, when he is considered simply as a man, with merely his own human conception of a doctrine of the faith. As Pope, as supreme teacher of the Catholic Church, he cannot err, when, by virtue of the assistance of God, promised and vouchsafed to him, he solemnly defines a truth revealed by God, and prescribes it to be held by the Universal Church. It is clear that there are in the one person of the Pope two different active powers (ἐνέργειαι): first, the ordinary power of thinking and viewing things;* and, secondly, the solemn defining power for the whole Church. I might illustrate this point by the parallel case of a judge who has to decide upon a suit. In his own private life he may, perhaps, hold and express his opinion, and that on very various occasions, but in the suit nothing passes for law but his solemn judicial utterance, which, however, is by no means infallible. The example, however, will suffice to show that a man who is invested with an official position can be readily conceived as thinking and speaking as a man, on the one hand, and, on the other hand, as an official personage in his forensic utterances and acts.

After making this distinction, plain enough as I conceive it to be, the introductory words of this Bull will be quite intelligible; why, that is, the Pope expresses his conviction how perilous it would be if, even in his private life, a Pope were to admit an error in doctrine, and what sad confusion would arise if the said Pope, as a private individual, were to be guilty of heresy, and yet had to put into force penalties against heretics, he as Pope having no judge higher than himself.†

* Of this ordinary faculty, Ballerini, in the passage we have already referred to, says very appropriately : 'Ex quo summi Pontifices ad Petri sedem promoti sunt, sicut non idcirco exuerunt humanam naturam, ita neque humanam agendi et opinandi rationem deposuerunt.'

† The question, 'an Papa, si in hæresim incidit (*i.e.* as *homo privatus*) deponi possit?' has been investigated and answered in different ways in former times. The introductory words of the

(9.) Dr. Schulte says further on, p. 35 : 'It is, moreover, quite an ordinary introduction to Bulls to find that the Pope is "Lord of the world," at least as far as it lies in his words and acts to make himself so.' So, for instance, says he, 'We find the *ex cathedrâ* (!) speaking Bull of Leo X. *Divina disponente*, in the eleventh session of the Fifth Lateran Council of Dec. 19, 1516, says Through the grace of God, . . Elevated on the high watch-tower of the Apostolate, and placed over peoples and lands,' &c.

Here, again, we have, according to Dr. Schulte, an *ex cathedrâ* speaking Bull. But what is it about? Why, it is really neither more nor less than the well-known Concordat between Pope Leo X. and King Francis I. of France.* This is the Concordat which for more than two centuries regulated the relations between Church and State, and which the kings of France themselves have so energetically upheld. And pray will any one be so good as to tell me when Concordats were first elevated to the rank of dogmatical decisions and utterances of the Pope *ex cathedrâ?* The honour of this discovery rests with Dr. Schulte. But will any one in sober earnest believe that the kings of France from the time of Francis I., kings who

Bull point to a solution of the difficulty in the sense of Pope Paul IV.; the real meaning of the words, however, depends on the right understanding of the word *redargui.*

* To be assured of this, we have only to look at the words with which the solemn reading of this Bull, in the eleventh session of the Fifth Lateran Council, is introduced. These are the words : 'Postmodum vero, Rev. Pater D. Maximus, Episcopus Iserniensis, ascendit ambonem et legit schedulam, in qua continentur *concordata* cum Christianissimo Rege Francorum. Cujus tenor sequitur, et est talis : Leo Episcopus, servus servorum Dei, etc. Divina disponente clementia,' &c. Harduin, *Acta Concil.* t. ix. Paris, 1714, col. 1809.

have been so jealous of the prerogatives of their crown, a Louis XIV., and other equally zealous sticklers for the rights of kings, would have been likely to be so mightily pleased with a Bull in which, according to Dr. Schulte's view, the Popes were called the Lords of the world? Or how comes it that Dr. Schulte has had the good luck to discover so dangerous a doctrine in this Bull, which for more than two centuries has escaped the observation of French kings and learned men? And now the truth must be told that Dr. Schulte has mutilated this Bull of a most essential portion of its introduction; for the real introduction runs as follows: 'By the grace of God, *through which kings rule and princes exercise authority*,* (the Pope) elevated on the high watch-tower of the Apostolate, and over peoples and lands,' &c. The words 'through which kings rule and princes exercise authority' (the very exact words whereby the temporal power of kings and princes is expressly acknowledged to be of divine grace), Dr. Schulte has thought fit to omit! I leave it to my readers to pass their own judgment on such mutilations and omissions.

(10.) Finally, in the last passage brought forward by Dr. Schulte from a Bull of Pope Sixtus V. in the year 1586, he stumbles on the following words: 'As the Roman Pontiff, the successor on the chair of Peter and true Vicar of Christ, holds by the divine preordination (*divina præordinatione*), the crown of the highest Apostolical dignity, and thus is in the place of Christ and of Peter upon earth; so the Cardinals of the holy Roman Church stand at the side of the Pope upon

---

* 'Divina disponente clementia, per quam reges regnant et principes imperant.' Harduin, *Acta Concil.* t. ix. Paris, 1714, col. 1809.

earth, representing the persons of the holy Apostles, as they served Christ our Lord, when He preached the Kingdom of God, and wrought out the mystery of the salvation of man.' On this passage he makes the following commentary: 'The theory is a simple one; the Pope is Peter; the Cardinals are the Apostles; *ergo*, the Catholic Church is wholly concentrated in the Roman Church. The Bishops, apart from the six Cardinal Bishops, are mere assistants. This, then, is the meaning of the third chapter of the dogmatic constitution of July 18, 1870' (p. 36 of Dr. Schulte's Pamphlet).

Strange that it should be now near three hundred years since Sixtus V. issued his Bull, and that we Bishops have, during all this time, never gained even an inkling from this Bull that we were no longer looked upon as the successors of the Apostles, and had been degraded to the position of mere assistants! The honour of this discovery also rests with Dr. Schulte. He seems not to be aware that as long ago as the time of St. Ignatius of Antioch, the immediate disciple of the Apostles, that holy Bishop says: 'Strive to do everything in union with God, under the presidency of the Bishop, who is in the place of God, and with the priests, who are in the place of the Council of the Apostles.'* If this great and renowned disciple of the Apostles thus spoke, then surely might Sixtus V. speak as he did. Moreover, the Bull of Pope Sixtus V. is not a definition *de fide*, not a Papal utterance *ex cathedrâ*; it is nothing more than a simple Bull for

* St. Ignatius, *Epist. ad Magnes*, c. vi. (*Patrum Apostolicorum Opera*, ed. G. Jacobson, Oxonii, tom. ii. p. 314); so often he speaks in like manner, *Epist. ad Trall.* c. iii. (ibid. p. 366); *Epist. ad Smyrn.* c. viii. (ibid. p. 430); *Epist. ad Philadelp.* c. v. (ibid. p. 394).

80   *It is 'de fide' that Bishops judge with the Pope.*

the organisation of the College of Cardinals, settling how many the number of the Cardinals ought to be, what qualifications those ought to have, who are to be taken into the high office of Cardinal, and the like.* Surely no sensible person will count as one of the doctrines of the Catholic Church how many Cardinals there ought to be, and what should be their qualifications? Moreover, to quiet all anxiety as to whether, from this Bull of 1586, the Bishops have lost their old privileges and their former dignity, we may bring forward what took place on April 24, 1870. On that day, in the third session of the Vatican Council, Pius IX. uttered the *de fide* definition: 'The Bishops of the whole world, gathered together with our authority in the Holy Ghost in this Ecumenical Synod' (they are the Pope's own words), '*sit* together with us, and give their *judgment* with us.' Just as was done in the Church of old. Well, then, from the year 1586 up to the year 1870, this Bull of Pope Sixtus had not deprived the Bishops of anything that belonged to their most important rights. There is here, however, just one point in which I find I can agree with Dr. Schulte —it is where he says ' that nobody compares a Papal utterance with the Gospel;' but then I do so on very different ground from him; my ground being that I am thoroughly convinced that there is no man living who would utter such a downright untheological absurdity as to compare a Papal utterance with the Gospel. The Gospel is, as is the complete Word of God, *inspired*

* See the Bull in question of Sixtus V., *Postquam Verus*, in the *Bullar. Rom.*, ed. cit. t. iv. p. iv. p. 279, where the contents of the title are given as follows: 'De S.R.E. Cardinalium creandorum præstantia, numero, ordine, ætate et qualitatibus, et de optione sex Cathedralium Ecclesiarum, quæ Cardinalibus conferuntur.'

by Him; that the Papal definitions *de fide*, infallible utterances *ex cathedrâ* as they are, are inspired by God, no one has ever taught, either in the Vatican Council or in the Catholic Church.

18. The FOURTH Proposition of Dr. Schulte is: 'The Pope has the right to bestow upon Catholic rulers lands and peoples who are not Catholic, and rulers so made may make them slaves.'

In proof of this he alleges: 'Pope Nicholas V., by his Bull *Romanus Pontifex*, as regards Western Africa, gave full leave to King Alphonsus of Portugal to take possession of all Saracens and heathen, and other enemies of Christ in all those parts, as well as of their kingdoms, and to make them their own inheritance,' &c. Now I hope it is, by this time, clear that a Bull giving over any temporal property, of any kind whatsoever, *is not* a Catholic article of faith; and of its being so there is not a trace in the Bulls cited by Dr. Schulte directed to King Alphonsus of Portugal.* Surely any man of ordinary abilities can distinguish between an infallible definition of faith and a certain course of conduct which, at a particular time and under particular circumstances, seemed proper for the extension of the Catholic faith amongst Turks and heathen; and this it is, which the Bulls quoted by Dr. Schulte are concerned with. And the case is the same in respect of all the Bulls quoted by Dr. Schulte under this fourth head, as any one may see who will be at the trouble of carefully reading these Bulls. But perhaps some of my readers may ask, 'Have the

---

* *Vide* Raynaldi, *Annal. Eccles.*, ad ann. 1443, n. 10-12; also ad ann. 1454, n. 8; and the Bull of Nicholas V., *Romanus Pontifex*, Jan. 8, 1454, in the *Bullar. Rom.*, ed. cit. tom. iii. p. iii. p. 70.

Popes really, in the fifteenth century, given away countries by virtue of their apostolical plenipotentiary authority?' To this I reply: It is not what Popes *do* in the plenitude of their authority, but what they *define* and teach by virtue of their supreme power of teaching in matters of faith, that is an utterance *ex cathedrâ*, and this it is which alone belongs to the question in hand. Here plainly is nothing whatever about a definition *de fide*.

19. The FIFTH Proposition of Dr. Schulte is: 'The Pope can enslave and bestow away those Christian subjects whose sovereign, or temporal superior, is under the anathema of the Pope.'

It would indeed be dreadful if, together with the definition *de fide* of the Vatican Council, delivered by the Infallible teaching authority of the Roman Pontiff, this was an article of faith which every Catholic, who hoped to be saved, was obliged to believe and obey. But if anybody has felt a qualm on reading this proposition, he may set his fears at rest. The case is not, after all, so desperate; it is only one of Dr. Schulte's self-invented Catholic *de fide* doctrines, of which the Catholic Church really knows nothing at all; it was invented by Dr. Schulte to horrify people, and to keep them from giving their assent to the real *de fide* doctrine on the Infallibility of the Pope in doctrinal definitions. This is the proof he gives of his proposition:

'It took place, and was declared by Pope Clement V., who in the year 1309, in a quarrel with the Venetians, excommunicated doge, senate, and people, declared them deprived of all rights, bade ecclesiastics refuse to exercise their office except in administering baptism and penance for the dying, confiscated all the possessions of the Venetians, and preached a crusade against them.*

Anybody may see that there is nothing here but a penal sentence,† which, however, Dr. Schulte has not even taken the trouble to give us correctly, as it is not the whole people who are excommunicated, and there is no mention of a crusade. But I will not be at the pains to enter into the correction of matters which are wholly irrelevant.

A similar penal enactment of Gregory XI. against the Florentines, in the year 1376, which he next mentions, belongs just as little to the province of Infallibility, and the same may be said of what he says about Adrian IV. and Paul III.

20. The SIXTH Proposition of Dr. Schulte is: 'The ecclesiastical laws upon ecclesiastical immunity, and upon Papal authority, rest upon divine inspiration.'

This is a very remarkable proposition. In proof of it, Dr. Schulte continues, ' Accordingly, Pope Julius II., in the fourth session of the Fifth Lateran Council, declares this, in the following words: "Julius, Bishop, servant of the servants of God, for a future memorial of this transaction, with the consent of the holy Council. Albeit, the dispositions of the holy Canons, of the holy Fathers, and Roman Pontiffs, our predecessors, and which have been sanctioned in legitimate‡ General Councils for the defence

* Raynal., *Annal. Eccles.*, ad ann. 1309, n. 6.*
† 'Judiciarium edictum,' as Raynaldus expressly and very properly calls it, t. xv. p. 43.
§ To these words Dr. Schulte appends the following remark: ' In generalibus legitimis Conciliis; a remarkable epithet! Are there, then, even General Councils which are only sham councils?' To prevent any one from being misled by this mischievous sugges-

of the freedom of the Church and its dignity, and for the protection of the Apostolic See, after mature deliberation must be held inviolate by all, and their decrees are esteemed unalterable, as if they had issued under divine inspiration," &c.'

Upon this proposition I have three remarks to make: first, the passages quoted from Pope Julius II. do not occur in a dogmatic definition, but in a 'peremptory judicial citation,'* and it is going a great way for any one to say that a judicial citation on a matter of discipline is to be regarded as an utterance *ex cathedrâ*. In the second place, Dr. Schulte would have done well to have quoted, not merely the preamble, 'Albeit the dispositions of the holy Canons are esteemed unalterable,' but also what follows in the preamble,† wherein we are told how far, nevertheless, the Pope *is* authorised to alter them. In the third place, it really is too bad that, when in the record quoted it is said, in the very words of the Pope,

---

tive question, I esteem it my duty to give the real reason of the word 'legitimis' being added. This we have plainly shown us in the Bull of Pope Leo X. *Pastor Æternus*, in the eleventh session of the Fifth Lateran Council. At that time there was an attempt to favour the Pragmatic Sanction by assuming the authority of the so-called General Council of Basle, to which title it had no claim after it had been displaced from the rank of General Councils. So the Synod of Pisa had falsely assumed the title ' Œcumenicum Generale atque Universale Concilium,' as we may see in the first session of the Fifth Lateran Council (Harduin, *Acta Concil.* t. ix. col. 1585). For this reason Leo X., in the Bull *Pastor Æternus*, already cited, says: ' Nullum infra hoc temporis spatium præter hoc Lateranense Concilium *legitime* fuisse celebratum.' Harduin, *Acta Concil.* t. ix. col. 1828.

* Monitorium contra Pragmaticam et ejus assertores. Harduin, *Acta Concil.* t. ix. col. 1642.

† ' Licet sacrorum canonum instituta . . . immutabilia censeantur,' are the words in the original text.

that the decrees of the canons are esteemed *as if* they were issued under divine inspiration, that Dr. Schulte, in his proposition, should omit this very expression, *as if*,* with all its important signification, simply saying, 'The laws of the Church upon ecclesiastical immunity and on Papal authority rest upon divine inspiration.'

21. The SEVENTH Proposition of Dr. Schulte is: 'The Church has the right to exercise an unconditional censure upon all writings.'

The Bull of Pope Leo X., issued in the tenth session of the Fifth Lateran Council, in the year 1515, *Inter Sollicitudines*,† serves as Dr. Schulte's proof for this.

This Bull is simply a disciplinary law with a penal threat, but is no definition on doctrine; this is clear for two reasons. The first reason is, that in the express words of the enactment in question the Pope says: 'That to restrain the bad results of a misuse of the invention of printing—a thing so good in itself, and so useful—he feels himself constrained to adopt certain regulations proper for the purpose' (*volentes de opportuno super his remedio providere*). This is not the way in which the Church utters her solemn definitions *de fide*. That, however, this enactment, which not the Pope alone, but the General Council of Lateran, had issued, belongs to the *alterable* discipline of the Church, the rescript of Pope Pius IX. of June 2, 1848, shows; in which important alterations are adopted in respect of this Bull of Pope Leo X.‡

---

* German 'gleichsam.' TRANSLATOR.
† Harduin, *Acta Concil.* t. ix. col. 1779.
‡ Pii IX. Pont. Max. Acta, pars i. pp. 99-101.

22. The EIGHTH Proposition of Dr. Schulte is: 'The Pope has the right to annul State laws, State treaties and constitutions, if they appear to him derogatory to the right of the Church and clergy.'

(1.) In proof of this, he brings the following: 'That he has power to annul laws generally is shown and maintained in the Bull *Pastor Æternus* of Leo X. Dec. 19, 1516, in the eleventh session of the Fifth Lateran Council, wherein the pragmatic sanction in France was rescinded under penalty of the greater excommunication.' (The pragmatic sanction is a kind of edict *de religione* of the fifteenth century.) Well, this is quite true, viz. that in this Bull of Leo X. the pragmatic sanction was annulled in France, but Dr. Schulte should not have kept his readers in ignorance that in this same Bull it is said in plain words that the King of France, Louis XI., had already previously annulled this same pragmatic sanction,* and that after this the Pope took from it all its validity on all points,† in an ecclesiastical point of view. This puts the matter in quite a different light, and we may well wonder how it came to pass

* For instance, Pope Leo says: 'Nos maturo attendentes, Pragmaticam Sanctionem a cl. m. Ludovico XI., Francorum Rege Christianissimo revocatam, cassatam atque abolitam.' Harduin, *Acta Concil.* t. ix. col. 1828. In the same way, Francis I. consents to the revocation of the Pragmatic Sanction, as is specially declared in the Concordat concluded between him and the Pope on the day specified, Dec. 19, 1516 (Harduin, *Acta Concil.* t. ix. col. 1812). Whoever desires to do so may find the curious old French original text of this Concordat in Andre's book, *Cóurs de Droit Canon*, Paris, 1853, t. ii. p. 168, where, from pp. 169-170 in the introduction to the Concordat itself, the removal of the Pragmatic Sanction by the two French kings, Louis XI. and Francis I., is circumstantially narrated.

† Why this was necessary Pope Leo X. explains in his Bull *Divina Disponente*, in Harduin, *Acta Concil.* t. ix. col. 1811.

that Dr. Schulte, who is so ready to bring before us the Acts of this Council, never saw this passage in them. I must not forget to add that, irrespective of all that has just been said, there is here no question of a definition *de fide* in the Bull. This anybody can see without any remark of mine.

(2.) The second proof of his proposition, which Dr. Schulte introduces after the following fashion, is as unfortunate as the first. 'Against one whole category of laws subjecting the clergy to the temporal jurisdiction, or taxing Church property, there are, as is admitted, innumerable Papal statutes, so that it is hard to make a selection. Some proofs will suffice from the so-called Bull *In Cœna Domini*.* "We curse and we damn—Lat. *excommunicamus et anathematizamus*†—all those who lay upon their country new burdens or taxes besides those which are due in equity, or which are imposed in particular cases by special Papal permission, all those who increase such taxes, or who impose new taxes, or who seek to revive those already forbidden."'

* *Bulla in Cœna Domini* is the name given to that Papal Bull which constitutes a kind of ecclesiastical penal statute in different important matters, and which was published in Rome every year on Holy Thursday, *Feria V. in Cœna Domini*, as a proof that it was still in force; hence the name. Like all human penal laws, it has undergone alterations from time to time. The penalty pronounced for the particular cases specified in the Bull was the penalty of excommunication. The copy of this ecclesiastical penal statute which Dr. Schulte brings forward belongs to the time of Paul V., 1610. It is in the *Bullar. Rom.*, t. v. p. iii. p. 393.

† It deserves to be noticed that Dr. Schulte translates the words of the Bull *excommunicamus et anatematizamus*, by the odious and, at the same time, incorrect formula, 'We curse and damn' (Ger. *verfluchen und verdammen*), instead of the correct translation 'We separate from the communion of the faithful and lay under anathema.'

Well, a simple ecclesiastical penalty is not a dogmatic definition, and, even if issued by the Pope, is not a Papal utterance *ex cathedrâ*.

Does not Dr. Schulte really know that this Bull has been cancelled now for a hundred years and more, and has ceased to be published on Holy Thursday?

And does he not know also that Pope Pius IX., in his Bull *Apostolicæ Sedis moderationi*, Oct. 12, 1869, has expressly declared that from that time only censures imposed *ipso facto* for certain cases were still to be held in force, and that all other ecclesiastical penalties of this kind were then revoked? The Pope at the same time gave his reason of this revocation of penalties in these words: 'These ecclesiastical penalties, which for security of the Church herself, and for the maintenance of her discipline, as well as for the restraint and improvement of the unbridled license of evil-disposed men, having been at different times issued with the most excellent intentions, have now become very numerous; and a portion of them, from altered times and altered habits of mind, having lost the object and the reasons for which they were introduced, have also lost their former usefulness and their applicability.'*

It is not a particularly happy line of argument

---

* 'Cum animo Nostro jam pridem revolveremus, ecclesiasticas censuras, quæ per modum latæ sententiæ ipsoque facto incurrendæ, ad incolumitatem ac disciplinam ipsius ecclesiæ tutandam, effrenemque improborum licentiam coercendam et emendandam sancte per singulas ætates indictæ ac promulgatæ sunt, magnum ad numerum sensim excrevisse, quasdam etiam, temporibus moribusque mutatis, a fine atque causis, ob quas impositæ fuerant, vel a pristina utilitate atque opportunitate excidisse.' So run the words of Pope Pius IX. in the Bull of Oct. 12, 1869.

that has to draw its proofs from the obsolete cancelled Bull *In Cœna Domini*, in order to demonstrate to the world what a Catholic has to believe and to accept, if he accepts the definition of the Vatican Council on the Infallible teaching office of the Roman Pontiff.

(3.) Dr. Schulte's third proof is drawn from the fact that Innocent X. in his Bull *Zelo Domus Dei* of the year 1648,* by virtue of his apostolical plenipotentiary power, declared the articles of the Peace of Westphalia, which were displeasing to him, to be null and void. First, I have to remark upon this, that the Pope did not declare the articles in question void as simply displeasing to himself, but as violations of the just rights of a third party. It was the duty of the Pope, as Head of the Catholic Church, to protect the rights of the Church in their full extent. For this purpose he here makes use of all the means afforded him by his spiritual office which circumstances admit of his using, such as earnest remonstrances, protests, or declarations of the infringement of his rights, and also ecclesiastical penalties, especially excommunication. It is undeniable that in the Peace of Westphalia, as well as in the acts of the Congress of Vienna in later times, the rights of the Church were in many ways violated. Against these violations of rights the Pope protests before God and before the world. He might, indeed, be pretty certain that the protest would be of little avail, but no fair inquirer will find fault with any one who has been despoiled of his rights for raising his voice and crying out aloud before God and men :† 'This spolia-

---

* *Bullar. Rom.*, ed. cit. t. vi. p. iii. p. 173.
† In this account there is no sort of contradiction between the Pope and the German Bishops, who seemed to sanction the Peace of

tion is invalid; I do not acknowledge it to be just.' A person who so acts is not to be branded as a disturber of the peace, and still less should be taunted with this when, after having given clear and manifest proofs of his rights, he showed that, in the interests of peace, he made no objection to come to terms with the despoiler.*

(4.) A further proof is drawn from the Austrian Concordat, because 'in this the Holy See gives its consent that in certain cases the secular court may pronounce judgment on spiritual matters and persons.'

It is inconceivable what this can have to do with the Infallibility of the Pope. And why upon earth is it to be considered a thing contrary to justice for the Pope to give his consent or permission to a change in an existing law of the Church? If even this is not allowed him, then, indeed, is the independence and autonomy of the Catholic Church come to an end altogether! A person who sanctions this simply wishes to annihilate the Church.

(5.) The Allocution of Pope Pius IX. June 22, 1868, after the fundamental State laws—the so-called confession laws—had been passed in Austria, is here brought forward by Dr. Schulte, because these laws were judged and partially condemned from an ecclesiastical point of view. But is it to be considered an

Westphalia by appealing to it. The Pope did *not* reject the *whole* of the treaty of the Peace of Westphalia, but only certain articles which were breaches of the rights of the Church. To these articles the German Bishops made no appeal.

* This is not the place critically to investigate whether the passage to which Dr. Schulte takes objection on this occasion is a purely imaginary fiction or not, viz. that the number 'seven' of prince-electors was established by apostolical sanction. Any one may see what can be said for it in Card. Bellarmine's *De Roman. Pontif.* lib. v. cap. viii.

infallible definition *de fide* that the Pope has expressed his own view of this matter? If not, why does Dr. Schulte introduce the subject at all? Surely the Pope had a right to ask for justice to be done him? Surely he might demand that a solemn concordat should be observed, which had been formally made in all its constituent parts? And as it was not observed, he, in his Allocution, protested against, rejected, and pronounced invalid, all that was contrary to the doctrine and to the rights of the Catholic Church; and in particular he protested against all that was contrary to the treaty that had been made. At a time when we hear complaints on all sides of broken treaties, why should we take it ill of the Pope that he, too, should oppose a breach of treaty with himself by such means as he had at his command?

(6.) Finally, Dr. Schulte rakes together several statements out of the Syllabus to serve as a proof of this proposition. These statements, however, are not given as in the words of the Syllabus, but in the form which a certain learned theologian has formulated the opposites of the rejected theses. But granting that this theologian is to be highly esteemed as a learned man, yet it is a generally received fact in the Catholic Church that the formulæ of Catholic theologians are not definitions *de fide*.

For the rest, Dr. Schulte assumes that the Syllabus, with all its eighty propositions, is one of those Papal definitions of doctrine of which the Vatican Council speaks in its fourth session. This assumption he has failed to prove. Dr. Schulte assumes it to be so as a *fact*, whilst the truth of the matter is, that this *fact* is called in question by the gravest theologians. Their doubt is founded especially upon this, that the form of the Syllabus is quite different from that which the Pope usually adopts when he delivers a solemn definition *de fide*. In order to convince himself of this, Dr. Schulte need only peruse the Bull of Leo X. against Luther, the *Exsurge Domine*, which he himself adduces as a Bull speaking *ex cathedrâ*, p. 27 of his book; or the celebrated Bull of Pius VI. *Auctorem Fidei*, August 28, 1794.* In these and in similar documents the intention of the Pope is expressed in the most decided manner, either at the beginning or at the end, that certain propositions must, by virtue of his supreme apostolical power, be regarded as incompatible with the Catholic doctrine on faith or morals. Now it is true that the propositions of the Syllabus are designated† in the title of the document as ' Errors of our time which the Holy Fathers have on different occasions denounced ;' but then it is certain that many of the documents in which a special error is denounced, and from which the propositions are drawn, are not utterances *ex cathedrâ*. But it may be said, perhaps, that the Pope, by requiring that the Syllabus should be made known to the whole Episcopate, desired to raise all his utterances on the errors contained in the Syllabus to the position of doctrinal definitions, such as would be, according to the definition of the Vatican Council, utterances *ex cathedrâ*. This many theologians think may be assumed to be doubtful, until a fresh declaration is made on the subject by the Holy See. For, as the Syllabus stands, neither the intro-

* *Bullarii Romani Continuatio*, t. ix. (Romæ, typis Rever. Cameræ Apost., 1845), p. 395, and following.

† The complete title of the Syllabus is : ' Syllabus complectens præcipuos nostræ ætatis errores qui notantur in Allocutionibus Consistorialibus, in Encyclicis aliisque Apostolicis litteris, SS. D. N. Pii Papæ IX.'

duction nor the conclusion is sufficiently clear upon this point. It is true the Bishops had an authentic announcement made to them through a letter of the Cardinal Secretary that the Syllabus was arranged and sent out at the command of the Holy Father, but the reason for this is given, and it comes to no more than this, that perhaps many persons would not be able to meet with the printed documents from which the propositions of the Syllabus are drawn. Certainly in the Papal Encyclical *Quanta Cura*, Dec. 8, 1864, which was promulgated with the Syllabus, it is said that Pius IX. has often raised his voice during his Pontificate against the principal errors of our time; but in that Encyclical there is nothing to show absolutely that the Pope in any one single word thought of the Syllabus.

23. The NINTH Proposition of Dr. Schulte is: 'The Pope has the right to reprove all temporal sovereigns, emperors, and kings for their misconduct, and on occasion to punish an offence *(in foro externo)*, as well as, in the case of a mortal sin, to bring it before the spiritual forum.'

In proof of this Dr. Schulte brings two passages from the book of Canon Law written by Popes.* The first of these is directed to the Grecian Emperor Alexius; the second to the French prelates, and concerns the King of France. Neither the one nor the other of these decretals is a definition *de fide*. No trace of a definition occurs therein. In both the Pope justifies his conduct towards the one and against the other of the two rulers mentioned, according to the

* C. Solitæ 6, de M. et O. (i. 33), and C. Novell. 13, de Judiciis, (ii. 1).

point of view common in the *Jus publicum* of those times.

24. The TENTH Proposition of Dr. Schulte is: 'Without the consent of the Pope no tax or impost can be laid upon any cleric or church.'

In proof of this Dr. Schulte brings forward a Bull of Boniface VIII., which, however, as he admits, was soon limited by Benedict XI., and afterwards entirely cancelled by Clement V. 'But,' he concludes, 'the Bull *In Cœna Domini* took up the matter, and in the Syllabus it is defined that Popes have never overstepped the limits of their powers.' I have already shown, No. 22 (2), that the Bull *In Cœna Domini* is now no longer in force; it is, in fact, entirely revoked. Dr. Schulte is thus left quite in the lurch, without the shadow of a reason for his assertion. His remark, by the way, 'In the Syllabus it is defined that Popes have never overstepped the limits of their powers,' does not help out his tenth proposition, and could only serve to strengthen the proof from the Bull *In Cœna Domini*. But as that Bull no longer exists, why, it follows that it cannot be strengthened.

Nor can it for a moment be admitted that the Pope *has* defined this in the Syllabus. The general assertion that the Popes have overstepped the limits of their powers is, indeed, mentioned amongst other errors. And the proposition, wherein it is laid to the charge of the Popes that they have in *general* overstepped the limits of their powers, is most justly condemned as erroneous. But that is a very different thing from a positive dogmatic definition that a Pope never in *any respect* overstepped the limits of his power.

25. The ELEVENTH Proposition of Dr. Schulte is: 'The Pope has the right to nullify the oath of allegiance taken to sovereigns whom he has excommunicated, and to forbid his subjects to obey him or his laws.'

In proof of this he brings forward the previously-mentioned Bulls of Gregory IX., Innocent IV., Paul III., and Pius V. Since however, as I have already shown, no one of these Bulls is a definition *de fide*, not an utterance *ex cathedrâ*, they do not belong to the subject in hand, and can constitute no proof that any one is obliged to receive the above-named proposition as a Catholic doctrine *de fide*.

26. The TWELFTH Proposition of Dr. Schulte is : 'The Pope can deprive excommunicate persons of all their social rights, and in particular can dissolve their marriages.'

(1.) The first proof of this is : 'Innocent IV. in his Bull *Cum adversus* of Oct. 31, 1243,* confirms the laws of the Emperor Frederick II. by accepting them. These laws condemn those guilty of heresy to the punishment of death at the stake; so in his Bull *Ad extirpanda* of May 15, 1243,† there follows a long list of punishments against heretics.' Here Dr. Schulte himself relieves me of the trouble of proving that there is here no definition *de fide*, no Papal utterances *ex cathedrâ*, by saying that 'the Pope only confirmed in the first of the rescripts, just mentioned, the penalties declared by Frederick II. against heretics.' This is the fact. And nothing could be a clearer

* *Bullar. Rom.* ed. cit. t. iii. p. 295.
† *Bullar. Rom.* ed. cit. t. iii. p. 324; where, however, this Bull bears date May 15, 1252.

proof than this, that there is no question in these rescripts of a definition on faith or morals ; for I fancy everybody knows now that imperial penal laws are not the place to seek for or to find Catholic doctrinal propositions. It ought to be mentioned, moreover, that this confirmation of the Pope was not issued for the whole Church, but expressly only for Lombardy, the Marches of Treviso, and the Romagna. Dr. Schulte's second Bull, that of Innocent IV., is wholly irrelevant as a dogmatic definition. It is designated simply a law, and nothing more. If I am asked the reason of this statement, I point simply to the wording of the Bull, which consists of thirty-eight paragraphs, each of which is noted down as 'Lex,' with the ciphering 'Lex 1,' 'Lex 2,' 'Lex 3,' &c. Surely this is sufficient proof. Moreover, this enactment is expressly limited by the Pope to Lombardy, the Romagna, and the Marches of Treviso. It really is difficult to characterise as it deserves such a mode of treating the subject under consideration. Dr. Schulte recklessly brings forward as infallible, and therefore unalterable definitions of doctrine issued for the whole Church, laws of Popes expressly made for particular occasions. The penal laws of the Popes against heretics, he has piled together in his notes, have nothing whatever to do with unalterable definitions of doctrine, but are examples of the spirit of the age in which they were passed, and of a discipline subject to change, but they in no way belong to the Infallibility of the Pope.

(2.) As a further proof of his proposition, he mentions the Bull of Paul IV., *Cum quorundam*, of Aug. 7, 1555,* in which Bull those several penalties

* *Bullar. Rom.* ed. cit. t. iv. p. i. p. 322.

which are usually pronounced only against relapsed heretics are pronounced also against those who deny certain specially named truths of the Catholic faith, as the doctrine of the Holy Trinity, the Divinity of our Lord Jesus Christ, &c. In his Bull there is no definition *de fide*, nothing but a simple penal law against certain persons who denied particular truths of the Christian faith which had been defined long ago. Here Dr. Schulte permits himself to digress into a violent sally on the subject of the irregularity* which, according to the ecclesiastical laws, is incurred by those who pronounce sentence of death, or those who carry the sentence into execution, and the different treatment which the Church adopts towards those who *pass a law* declaring the sentence of death for certain offences, and the judge who *condemns* to death in virtue of that law. When he here calls the Church's action ' a fiction to stifle the conscience,' and nicknames it 'Pharisaism,' he writes without knowing what he writes about. The irregularity spoken of is not *ex delicto*, but *ex defectu*; it is not incurred because the person who pronounces a just judgment has committed any sin which might burden his conscience. It is only in case of a man committing sin that the reproach of ' stifling the conscience' has any meaning, or that the word 'Pharisaism' is at all applicable. Irregularity *ex defectu lenitatis* was introduced by the Church, because the Church did not think it a proper or seemly thing that one who, even in the most just manner, had been brought into immediate contact with the death of a human being,

* The word ' irregularity' is known to theologians as a technical word, denoting an impediment as regards ordination or the exercise of the sacred ministry.

be it by the condemnation of him, or by the execution of the sentence, should receive or exercise the office of Holy Orders. How far this respect for the dignity of the clerical office should be extended depends upon considerations which have nothing to do with sin.

(3.) Finally, as his last reason, Dr. Schulte brings forward, 'The conduct of Pope Urban V. towards Bernard Visconti, Duke of Milan, in the year 1363. As the matter is pictured to us by historians, he ordered his condemnation to be published, whereby he declared him a heretic, infidel, and schismatic, anathematised by the Church; he freed his subjects from their oath of allegiance, and his wife as a Christian from her marriage contract with a man who was a heretic and an infidel.'

Here we have before us, as Dr. Schulte himself says, only a sentence of condemnation against a prince who was deserving of punishment, not a definition *de fide.* Surely he is not going to make all judicial sentences which the Popes have pronounced for many hundred years past do duty as utterances *ex cathedrâ?* In this case such decisions would be innumerable. Canonist as he is, he cannot mean to assert this in sober earnest. Besides, we may justly demand that the exact words of the sentence should be produced, in which the Pope, contrary to the clear and express directions of the ecclesiastical law, dissolved the marriage tie on account of heresy. Without this we cannot consider so grave an accusation against a Pope. Instead of this sentence we have only the casual words of a late historian, Spondanus, and we are not told whether *he* ever really saw the sentence himself, or only reported it second-hand. It would be waste of time to enter upon an exposition of the true meaning of a judicial sentence when the words used are of so·much importance, and when we do not know what those words were.*

In Raynaldi's great work mention is indeed made of the terms of this sentence, but the words respecting the dissolution of the marriage tie do not occur there.†

27. Finally, the THIRTEENTH Proposition of Dr. Schulte is: 'The Pope can release from an obligation (as of oath and vow) both before and after the oath or vow has been taken.

'Proved,' he says, 'by the *Privilegium* which Clement V. gave to King John of France and his consort, and to all his successors, that all and every one of their father confessors, whether secular or regular, might dissolve and commute, for works of piety, all vows which they have already taken, and all which either they or their successors might take in future,‡ as well as all oaths which they had already taken, or which they or their successors might hereafter take, and change them into works of piety.' But no one

---

* In this uncertainty about the passage on which the proof is based there can be no real question of a contradiction between the penal sentence of Urban V., in the year 1363, and the later dogmatic definition of the Council of Trent in the year 1563; and thus the scornful remark of Dr. Schulte comes to nothing. His remark is on p. 50 of his Pamphlet : 'Thus it follows that Urban V., with the consent and in the presence of the College of Cardinals and of the Roman Church, passed a fearfully solemn act against a proposition *de fide*. How, in the face of such an instance as this, can people plume themselves on their invention of the phrase *ex cathedrâ !*'

† Raynaldi, *Annal. Eccles.* ad ann. 1363, n. 2, t. xvi. p. 423.

‡ Here follow three exceptions, which I omit for brevity's sake.

says that Papal Privilegia* are infallible definitions *de fide*. And if they are not this, then they do not belong to the matter on hand. Faculties to commute vows into other works of piety are still reserved to the Pope. As regards oaths;—in the case of an oath by which a promise is confirmed, where the oath ought not to be kept, but where the person, to whom something has been promised on oath, insists on the fulfilment of the promise, there a Catholic has the option of referring the decision either to the Pope, or to his father confessor, or he may decide for himself whether this is really a case in which obligation to stand by the oath ceases. Should a case occur in which the obligation to the observance of an oath ceases, as for instance when its observance would lead to the violation of some moral duty, then it would be unadvisable to leave the decision to the person himself who has made the oath, as he often has an interest in the dissolution of the oath.† For the rest, it is to be observed that the Pope, in granting this privilege to the confessor so chosen, does not give an unlimited power to commute vows and oaths into works of piety, as Dr. Schulte asserts, but only vows and oaths which a person cannot observe, according as the confessors for the time being judge to be desirable for the good of the souls intrusted to them.‡ This last part of the document

* 'Privilegia quædam regibus Franciæ impertita,' in D'Achery's *Spicilegium*, Paris, 1723, is the correct title of a long list of such documents as we now call faculties received from the Pope. They are dispensations from fasting, indulgences, permissions respecting Masses, absolutions *in foro externo*, &c.

† And this is why such an oath is referred to the Pope, because he is an impartial judge. TRANSLATOR.

‡ 'Prout secundum Deum et animarum vestrarum et eorum saluti viderit expedire.'

Dr. Schulte has entirely omitted. That, moreover, this faculty should be exercised on such vows and oaths as were not yet in existence at the time of the grant of the privilege is just as natural as that, when a Bishop nowadays gives a priest power to absolve from sins for a period of four years, he should not limit this power of absolving to sins which have already been committed, but should give power to absolve sins which, in the course of one, two, or three years, may hereafter be committed and confessed.

The example adduced by Dr. Schulte of the nullification of an oath by Paul IV., A.D. 1555, will serve as confirmation of the explanation I have given: 'the Pope,' he says, 'in the case of an unlawful oath expresses his will to release the emperor, and declare him free from his obligation.'* But a release from an oath, which the Pope has thought good to make in a particular case, has never yet been regarded by any one as an infallible utterance *ex cathedrâ*.

We have now arrived at the conclusion of Dr. Schulte's alleged Papal doctrinal propositions and acts. The result of the whole investigation has been that the passages which he has brought forward as his proofs are not such expressions as are to be regarded as utterances *ex cathedrâ*, that is as infallible definitions on the Catholic faith or morals.† Accordingly a Catholic who accepts on

* It should here be noticed that the authority for this mere oral utterance of the Pope, Bzovius, (*Annal. Eccles.* ad ann. 1555, n. 36, Coloniæ, 1640, t. xx. p. 306) does not mention the record from which he drew his information; so this *presumed* Papal utterance is of a somewhat imaginary character.

† The Bull *Unam Sanctam* alone forms an exception to this statement, but not even that Bull is an exception in its full extent, as Dr. Schulte asserts. See above, no. 16.

faith, in accordance with his obligation, the definition *de fide* of the Vatican Council on the Infallible teaching office of the Roman Pontiff, is in no way obliged to believe these thirteen propositions, which I have given word for word from his work, to be infallible utterances.

CHAPTER III.
Second Part.

RELATION OF POPES TO THE STATE-LAW. TREATMENT OF HERETICS.*

28. OUR task as regards the principal question is now discharged. But as, for the quieting of my reader's conscience and to enable him to see his duty clearly, I undertook to discuss not the principal question only—whether a Catholic in accepting the Vatican definition is in reality bound to accept these thirteen propositions as articles of faith—but also to examine any other incidental questions which might arise out of the expressions and doings of Popes to which our attention has been directed, I will now briefly discuss this second question. It resolves itself into two heads, to which these Papal expressions and acts refer: first, 'the relation of Popes to the State;' and secondly, 'their treatment of heretics.' Now as regards the relation of Popes to the State we must bear in mind that all the expressions and acts of the Popes towards the State which have been mentioned in the principal propositions occur in the period from the eleventh to the sixteenth century. Hence it follows:

(1.) The *Jus publicum*, as it was then laid down and acknowledged, must be accepted as furnishing us with the means of forming a right judgment of the precedents which took place in this period.

(2.) This *Jus publicum* was founded upon the general understanding, then prevalent, that European

* Translator's heading.

Christendom was based on the principles of the Catholic religion and derived its stability from it.

(3.) Accordingly, a man who did not belong to the Catholic Church could hold no position in public life.

(4.) Every one who was invested with any public office was obliged to direct his life according to the doctrines and principles of the Catholic religion.

(5.) If he did not do this, he fell under the penal authority of the Church and of the State.

(6). The penal authority of the Church was, in its supreme instance, exercised by the Popes, who being independent, did justice fearlessly, even against the great and mighty of this world.

(7.) Nor must it here be left out of consideration what an important influence the laws of the old Roman Empire, Justinian's code, and the 'Novellæ' exercised in the West, and how many and what important rights ('jura') were conceded to the Church by means of these old Roman statutes.*

(8.) Nothing can give plainer evidence of the prevailing opinion in those times with regard to the *Jus publicum* in social life than the fact that kings

---

* *Vide* Savigny's *History of the Roman Law in the Middle Ages*, 2d edit. vol. iii., Heidelberg, 1834, p. 87, where he says : 'As far back as from the times of Charlemagne it had been the custom to look upon a large portion of the European nations and states as in one lasting alliance, and to assume a solidarity even in, it might be, that special thing which distinguished them one from another. In this range of matters common to all were comprised "The Imperial Power," "The Roman Catholic Church Constitution," "The Clerical State," "The Latin, the language of all social transactions ;" and under this category fell also "The Roman Statute Law," which was considered not as the special law of any Roman province nor even as the private law of any particular State, but as *the common Christian European law*.'

again and again had recourse to the Popes to obtain their judgment on a matter.* Had this practice not been grounded in the *Jus publicum* of the time, the Emperor Frederick II. would never have undertaken to defend himself at the first general council of Lyons before Pope Innocent IV., through his plenipotentiary ambassador, in order to escape the Pope's condemnation. This shows how fully he recognised the Pope's right.

(9.) According as this great family of nations brought out in different ways its internal conviction that its social life rested on a Catholic foundation, and must be penetrated through and through and guided by the Catholic truth, so it considered it its duty to spread everywhere the knowledge of the Christian Catholic religion.

(10.) Temporal dominion was undoubtedly everywhere recognised as ordained by God.†

These, then, we find to be (1) the generally received views of law (jus) in that period, but these views are in no sense (2) Papal definitions of faith made for all periods till the end of time.

These two things, then, must be kept quite distinct.

* The decretal of Pope Innocent III. may serve as an example of this, in cap. 13, Novell. De Judiciis, whence we see that the King of England cited the King of France before the Pope in order to have right done to him. *Vide* also c. 15, De Foro Competenti, ii. 2.

† Pope Innocent III. in his decretal, *Solitæ*, c. 6, De M. et O., i. 33, says this expressly in the following words : 'Ad firmamentum igitur cœli, hoc est, universalis ecclesiæ fecit Deus duo magna luminaria, id est, duas instituit dignitates, quæ sunt Pontificalis auctoritas et regalis potestas.' This may serve as a confutation of Dr. Schulte's false proposition, as though the Popes had taught 'the temporal power is from the wicked one.' P. 29 of his work.

Here I am going to take the liberty to introduce a passage which bears upon this subject from an historical work of one of our most celebrated German authors, which will, I think, tend to throw light on our subject, and enable us to see it in its true proportions. The writer is Frederick Hurter. In his history of Innocent III., having made a thorough investigation of the records of that time, he says: 'The Church was the source of all higher social life in the human race; hence in her there was safety, outside of her there was no safety. In her mission, which was to include the whole world, in order to bring all people of the earth to the knowledge and adoration of the true God, he who was at the head of the Church was compelled, as his most sacred obligation, to bring into her dominion those who were afar off, to remove those who had separated from her, and so had to consider that the gain of those who entered into the great hospice of salvation was of more importance to themselves than to the Church.' (Book II.)

Again: 'The Church secured the Empire against that absolutism which will not endure by its side any law but its own. The veneration of the Empire for the Church procured that universal recognition of her in all countries, without which Christendom would have been abandoned to the separatist influence of ideas, customs, and inclinations of peoples, and split asunder into ever so many sects, or perhaps have become the property of a school. But so (by this mutual support) it formed itself into that bond of union which embraced the nations, which sustained their social life, promoted civilisation, and maintained the spiritual rights of all, and enabled the Christian

West, as one whole in living faith, to sustain the shock of the Mahometan East, which was contending with it for the empire of the world in all the fresh vigour of a doctrine kindled by human passion.' (Book II.)

Again: 'There lay in Christendom for all its votaries a uniting and a binding power. The rights of all were put under its protection, the duties of all were marked out and consecrated by it. He who stood at the head of the great Christian community had to protect some, and yet to be mindful of others.* And thus there was founded a world-government which gave due honour to each lawful authority when moving in its own proper sphere.'

Again: 'If ever the dream of a universal peace is to be realised, it can only be possible by the general acknowledgment of some one spiritual power, raised above all others, to investigate and smooth the way in the strifes of kings and peoples, to mediate and to adjust; and when that king or nation shall be treated as the common enemy, who, trusting in his own strength, shall refuse to acknowledge the decisions of this supreme spiritual power.' (Book XX. Hurter's *History of Innocent III.*)

29. In close connection with this stands the treatment of heretics in that period.

* This passage recalls the words of a French philosopher which may interest our readers: 'Est-ce un si grand mal de rappeler aux princes mêmes leurs devoirs et les droits des nations lorsqu'ils les oublient ? Qui réclamera donc en faveur des peuples, si la religion, cette seule et unique barrière, qui nous reste contre le despotisme et le désordre, se tait ? N'est pas à elle à parler, lorsque les lois gardent le silence ? Qui enseignera la justice, si la religion ne dit rien ? Qui vengera les mœurs, si la religion est muette ? En un mot, de quoi servira la religion, si elle ne sert à réprimer le crime ?'

The Catholic Church and heresy are, in their own nature, and in the mind of the Church, antagonistic as truth and error.

I mean, in the mutual relation they hold one to the other as regards the inner self of both the one and the other.

Externally, however, we find that in the course of centuries the Church has adopted a very different conduct towards heretics, according to the different circumstances in which she has been placed in her intercourse with the world.

Thus we may distinguish four different periods.

The 'First Period' reaches from the commencement of the Christian era to the first decade of the fourth century. During this time, in treating with heretics, Christians acted according to the words and examples of the Apostles. What this way was, the Apostle Paul told the faithful: 'A man that is a heretic, after the first and second admonition avoid, knowing that he that is such an one is subverted and sinneth, being condemned by his own judgment' (Titus iii. 10, 11). And the Apostle John says: 'If any man come to you and bring not this doctrine, receive him not into your house, nor say to him, God speed you' (2 John v. 10). This is the way in which the early Catholics protected themselves from heretics; they excluded them from their communion, and, in some cases, even broke off intercourse with them in order that they might not be corrupted by their errors.

The 'Second Period' begins with the First Council of Nicæa, A.D. 325, at which time the Christian rulers of the Roman Empire sent the principal teachers of error into banishment* from political reasons, and in order to prevent their doing mischief, because there was good reason for considering them disturbers of the public peace; and severe fines and other punishments were imposed on those who were the disciples of their errors. This period lasted for some centuries, as long as the Roman law was in force.

In the 'Third Period,' that of the Middle Ages, rulers went farther; fines were not only followed by confiscation of goods, but even capital punishment or imprisonment for life was pronounced against heretics, and this by the imperial laws of the Emperor Frederick II.† and other emperors; to these laws the Popes were a party, as Leo X.‡ expressly testifies. At that time, people looked upon heresy as a breach of the imperial law, to be punished with the loss of honour, forfeiture of goods, deprivation of civil rights, &c. Testimony of this is expressly given by Frederick II., who declares that in punishing heretics, he was but exercising his own temporal power, wholly independently, and was not acting under the influence of any spiritual authority. The reason the emperor gives for inflicting such heavy penalties was because it was a greater breach of the law to offend against the Divine Majesty than against

---

* In this way Arius, and the few Bishops who had voted against the majority of 318, in the definition of faith made at that Council, were sent into banishment by the Emperor Constantine, as was also, later on, Nestorius: see Sozom. *Hist. Eccl.* lib. i. c. xx. xxi.; Philostorgii, *Hist. Eccl.* lib. i. n. 9, 10; Evagrii, *Hist. Eccl.* lib. i. c. vii. ed. Vales; Cod. Theodos. *De Hæreticis* (xvi. 5), l. 13, 14, 19, 30, 31, 32, 33, 34, 45, 52, 54, 64, ed. Ritter, t. vi. p. i. Lipsiæ, 1743.

† Vide Pertz, *Mon. Germ. Legum*, t. ii. pp. 287, 288.

‡ Vide Bull *Exsurge Domine*, *Bullar. Rom.* t. iii. p. 488.

any earthly majesty. This was the general way of viewing men's public social relations at that time. This Period lasted till well on into the sixteenth century.

The 'Fourth Period,' which has been running its course up to the present time from the seventeenth century, did away with those penal enactments which had been passed under very different circumstances, as the reasons which had led to their being enacted, and the principles on which they rested, were no longer in force since the establishment of Protestant States in Europe. This is the period in which we meet with only protests or the reservation of rights, when, that is, the rights of the Church, whether divine, or legal, or accruing to her from contract, were violated in favour of heretics.

CHAPTER IV.

'PLEAS DEVISED TO QUIET THE CONSCIENCE, AND THEIR CONFUTATION.'*

30. IT is in this section of his Pamphlet that Dr. Schulte shows us most clearly that the position in which he places himself with regard to the Vatican definition is the very reverse of mine. I will endeavour to point out the contrast.

We both begin by taking for granted that the whole controversy originates in the *de fide* definition of the Vatican Council, on the Infallible teaching office of the Roman Pontiff. Out of this definition he deduces the following proposition, which, however, he omits to define more accurately: 'What the Popes have declared to be the doctrine of the Church, that is true, and must be believed and followed in practice by all Catholics.'

To this he appends a long list of Papal declarations drawn from documents of the most different kind—briefs, laws, concordats, citations, penal judgments, &c.

Of these documents he asserts that, if a person receives the Vatican definition, they must, one and all, be regarded by him as Papal definitions, must be believed in and followed in practice.

---

* It must not be forgotten that Bishop Fessler places at the head of his chapters the titles of the very chapters of Dr. Schulte which he refutes. The 'Pleas' here spoken of are the replies supposed to be made by Ultramontane defenders of Infallibility, not Fessler himself, to the view maintained by Dr. Schulte. TRANSLATOR.

The reply, that this is an incorrect statement, and that, in stating his proposition so generally, he has started with an error, which has led him into further erroneous assertions and conclusions, he turns aside by saying, that 'such pleas are merely devised to quiet the conscience.'

This, then, is his position.

Mine, however, has been: (1) To lay plainly before my readers the Definition; (2) to weigh carefully its wording and its sense; and (3) to give my reflections upon it; and I say that these reflections show us plainly that the utterances of the Pope are to be received as infallible definitions only under certain conditions, and that these conditions have been exactly specified in the Vatican Council itself.

Dr. Schulte, in presenting for our consideration numerous Papal expressions and Papal doings which he himself regards as so many infallible utterances, has enabled us to see that, with one single exception,* the conditions which the Vatican Council has declared to be requisite for an infallible definition, are not to be found in these documents which he parades before us, and therefore that all the Papal expressions and Papal acts, therein spoken of, cannot, according to the Vatican definition, come into the class of infallible Papal definitions.

This I consider that I have demonstrated, and I am compelled to say, that what Dr. Schulte really means by the term 'pleas devised to quiet the conscience,' is the *true* and *essential* meaning of the definition of the Vatican Council, and this is of itself sufficiently remarkable. By using this term he refuses to allow the validity of those essential restrictions by which the Infallibility

* Part of the Bull *Unam Sanctam*.

of the Pope is limited, as it is necessary it should be, in order that the true Catholic doctrine on faith and morals may be preserved in its purity.

Such a proceeding on the part of a learned Catholic professor must meet with the most decided condemnation of the whole Catholic Church. How can a man, who lays claim to the name of Catholic, venture to say of a definition of an Ecumenical Council, that its essential restrictions are mere 'pleas to quiet the conscience'?

31. As the first of these 'pleas to quiet the conscience,' Dr. Schulte brings forward the distinction which has been drawn between the Pope acting as a *private person*, but not as *Pope*, and that it is admitted that he may possibly, as a private person, have erred in commanding, or in directing by law, something which cannot be justified.

Here I must remark first, that nobody really has the folly to assert, as Dr. Schulte lays to the charge of the advocates of Papal Infallibility, that they say, ' The Pope may, as a private person, have commanded, or directed by law, something which cannot be justified.'

The first step then in a controversy, in order to relieve yourself of the burden of a proof, is to find out some nonsense, lay that nonsense on your adversary's shoulders as a target, and then discharge your weapons at it!' What we really do say is,—that the Pope may err as a private person, and as such may give utterance to his error (cf. above, No. 17 (8)); not that he can either command, or by law direct, anything to the Church 'as a private person.'

Dr. Schulte proceeds further to say: 'It is beyond all doubt that every proceeding which the

Pope has ever taken in hand, or which he now takes in hand, relating to the province of his teaching office or to Church government, is really not the act of a private person, *x*, but is the act of the Pope *as* Pope, and that the Pope acts *as* Pope, whether the act in question is an act done for the diocese of Rome or for some other diocese, or for the whole Church. But this conclusion which he draws is by no means so certain as he assumes it to be. For the sake of brevity, I will but refer to one of the greatest authorities in the Catholic Church, viz. the learned Pope Benedict XIV., who asserts the very contrary, a fact which may at least be permitted to make Dr. Schulte's view somewhat doubtful.*

This Pope says in his preface to his celebrated work, *De Synodo Diœcesanâ*, published at the time when he actually was Pope, that 'In this work he

* For instance, Pope Benedict XIV. says: 'Romanus Pontifex qui (according to Theodorus Studita) est omnium Capitum Caput, atque Christi Ecclesiæ Princeps, Moderator et Pastor, est etiam Patriarcha Occidentis, Primas Italiæ, Archiepiscopus et Metropolitanus Romanæ Provinciæ, atque Episcopus urbis Romæ ; quod scite considerant, Sirmondus, Morinus, Leo Allatius, Hallier, Natalis Alexander, et passim alii. Non inde tamen, quod Romanus Pontifex insitam sibi habeat dignitatam et prærogativam supremi Capitis totius Ecclesiæ, consequitur, omnia, quæ ab eo fiunt, fieri tanquam ab Ecclesiæ Capite, siquidem aliquando solum gerit personam vel Primatis Italiæ, vel Metropolitæ Romanæ Provinciæ, quandoque se tantum exhibet Episcopum urbis Romæ, ea unicè peragendo, quæ cuilibet Episcopo in suâ diœcesi peragendi jus est ; aliquando demum suam supremam explicat dignitatem, et tanquam totius Ecclesiæ Præses, Moderator et Princeps illam exercet potestatem et jurisdictionem, qua non nisi ut Christi in terris Vicarius potitur. Neque quod quis pro loco et tempore diversas induat personas, et modo unâ modo alterâ ex iis utatur potestatibus, quibus diverso nomine præstat, res est adeo nova et inusitata, ut ab heterodoxis irrideri queat.' P. Benedict XIV. *De Synodo Diœcesanâ*, lib. li. cap. i. Ferrariæ, 1760, pp. 29, 30.

desires to *define* nothing in respect of that for which he does not adduce Papal definitions, even if he expresses his own view upon the subject (*sententiam Nostram proponentes*), just as his great predecessor, Innocent IV., expressed his own opinions only as a private person and scholar* in the commentary he published upon the Decretals, adding also that this was the view he wished to be generally taken of his commentary.' Surely from this it is pretty clear that the distinction, which Dr. Schulte casts aside as mere words, has been so long known and is so well founded in the Church, that I may spare myself any further explanation of it.

32. Dr. Schulte next brings forward the following proposition as his second instance of a 'plea devised merely to keep people's consciences quiet:' 'The Council decrees Infallibility to belong only to utterances which have reference to doctrine, of faith, or morals, but that Infallibility has nothing to do with legislating or governing.'

In the somewhat lengthy discussion upon this proposition there is a regular torrent of repetitions of propositions and assertions already brought forward in previous pages of his pamphlet, all of which have been examined one by one, and as I think sufficiently refuted. So I might content myself with referring my reader to what I have already said, since I must take care how I weary him by a repetition of what has been already sufficiently refuted. I think, however, it may be worth while just to extract the principal propositions out of this part of Dr. Schulte's pamphlet, and to set them in their proper light, so far as there is

---

* 'Opiniones suas quas tanquam privatus Doctor proposuerat.' P. Benedict XIV. In Proœmio, op. cit. p. ix.

anything new in them, which might possibly perplex and trouble some of the less observant of his readers. He has, he tells us, collected them all together in this part of his treatise, in order to show that the Catholic Church at the Vatican Council *could not* possibly define the Infallibility of the Pope *only* in that limited sense in which it did define it, viz. as having reference only to doctrine respecting faith and morals (p. 53 of his pamphlet).* This new assertion of his Dr. Schulte endeavours to prove out of Holy Scripture, and from the nature of the Primacy. Strange position for a man to claim for himself! He understands the nature of the Primacy better than the Primate himself and the 500 bishops. He says that in Holy Scripture there is not a word of any special teaching office of St. Peter, and he adds, 'the Vatican Council has not been able to appeal in its definition to any such passage.' But however Dr. Schulte may deny this, the Council *has* appealed to such a passage, and that passage contains the words

* This also is the place to state Dr. Schulte's view, 'that the *ex cathedrâ* theory is a mere invention of the schools and has no foundation either in itself, and is utterly worthless in law.' One cannot but be surprised at hearing a learned man speak so recklessly and contemptuously of the science of theology. For the term *ex cathedrâ*—by which is meant that sometimes the Pope speaks *ex cathedrâ* and sometimes not, and that *ex cathedrâ* utterances have quite a different import from those statements which are not *ex cathedrâ*—is a conclusion arrived at by the science of theology; and since the formula has been received by the Church, it has as much claim on our acceptance as is possessed by any older formula or expression, which although not in Scripture, and not in use in the first centuries, has nevertheless been selected by the Church, when making a solemn *de fide* definition in later times, as the most appropriate term to designate a definition *de fide*. Instances of this kind of formulas are well known to all theologians.

of our Lord to St. Peter, 'I have prayed for thee that thy faith fail not; and do thou in turn one day strengthen thy brethren.'* This passage is taken from St. Luke xxii. 32, and to this passage the Vatican Council expressly refers by quoting it *verbatim* in the definition.

33. Again, Dr. Schulte asserts, 'It will not do, on the one hand, to base the Infallibility upon the Primacy of the Roman Bishop, and at the same time, on the other hand, to exclude from the operation of Infallibility the giving of laws and all other Papal acts, except mere theoretical doctrinal definitions' (p. 54).†

(1.) Upon this I remark that, since the supreme power has various operations in the Church, God hath vouchsafed to its one most important operation a special grace. I call the teaching office the most important operation, because it is by teaching that faith comes, and because the right faith is the foundation of the whole work of salvation in man; as also for this reason, because teaching is the guide, the *norma*, both as regards the sacraments, and as regards the giving of laws and governing. The truth of salvation, revealed by God and preserved from error, is the foundation of all the other operations which the Church exercises for the salvation of man. Herein lies the reason for the possibility and for the fitness of

* See Preface, conclusion, for the reason why Bishop Fessler adopted this translation. TRANSLATOR.

† We call our readers' attention to this expression, 'mere theoretical doctrinal definitions.' If Dr. Schulte means to say or imply that such *theoretical* acts are of no importance, he is greatly to be blamed. The faith of a Catholic is directed by such definitions of doctrine, and his life by his faith,—'Justus ex fide vivit.' Rom. i. 17; Galat. iii. 11; Heb. x. 38.

the gift of a special grace to the highest teaching power in the Church,—viz. to exclude thereby all error from the doctrines of the Church. That this gift has actually been conferred, rests on the words of Christ as they are given us in Holy Writ, according to the declaration and tradition of the Holy Church. Thus, then, from this true doctrine disciplinary laws are deduced through the operation *of man*; in accordance with this true doctrine the Church is governed; and thus, in both discipline and government, we confidently hope and believe that the divine assistance is not wanting to the Pope.

From this we see the wisdom of the Church's action, that on the one hand all her definitions of faith should be unalterable, and that on the other hand, it should be lawful for bishops to make representations as regards Papal disciplinary laws, even when they have been issued for the whole Church—if, that is, they have reason to fear that such and such laws would have a prejudicial effect on their subjects in some way or other—in order that special alterations, exceptions in behalf of particular countries or regions, relaxations of penalties, &c., may be brought into action.*

Further, it is admitted that these laws may be entirely set aside, under certain conditions, after a proper length of time has elapsed, by a legitimate

---

* So Pope Benedict XIV. *De Synodo Diœces.* lib. ix. c. viii. nn. 1 and 3, where he speaks in quite a different manner on the one hand—' De Pontificiis Constitutionibus, quæ ad fidem pertinent, cum in his irreformabile sit Romani Pontificis judicium'—from what he does on the other, 'De Constitutionibus ad disciplinam pertinentibus,' in respect of which last he expressly concedes the right of bishops to make representation about them, in order to obtain alterations.

contrary custom.* How and why on certain occasions even the formal revocation or partial modification of laws passed in former times can be effected by Popes themselves, has already been shown above in a striking example (No. 22, p. 86).†

(2.) Dr. Schulte endeavours to help on his cause by saying that several of the Papal constitutions which he has brought forward under the head of Papal doctrinal propositions have certainly reference to the faith, as for instance 'Laws against heretics refer to the propagation of the faith' (p. 57 of his pamphlet), or, as he says in another place (p. 59), 'a number of such constitutions belong exclusively to the faith.' This assertion, however, rests on a mere play of words. Of course, it may be said, in a certain sense, penal enactments and condemnations of heretics do refer to the faith, because they punish a lapse from the faith. But the definition of faith of the Vatican Council says expressly Infallibility is promised to the Pope if he defines a dogma on faith or morals (*doctrinam de fide vel moribus definit*). Who does not see that it is quite a different thing for the Pope to pronounce a definition upon a doctrine of the Church on faith or morals, and to direct or apply this or that means in order to protect people from falling away from the Catholic faith, or to bring back or punish those who have fallen from it? The first belongs to the teaching office, the latter to jurisdiction.

(3.) Hereupon Dr. Schulte tries another shift; he says, 'It is from these Papal laws and acts of Papal

* P. Benedict XIV. *De Synod. Diœcesanâ*, lib. xiii. cap. v. nn. 4-5.

† Any one who is well acquainted with Papal Bulls of the sixteenth and seventeenth centuries will recall a great number of examples of this sort.

governments that we can learn the principles upon which the Popes have acted, as they have taken them for granted in making their laws and when acting as rulers of the Church; thus these laws and acts are after all real definitions on Church doctrine.' To this I answer, granting even that we can draw more or less certain conclusions out of Papal laws and acts of Papal governments as to the principles to which such laws owe their origin, yet we are by no means justified in viewing these principles so inferred, as the definitions on faith and morals of which the Vatican Council is speaking in its definition on Infallibility.

By that definition it was clearly meant to make definitions of the Pope *ex cathedrâ* as plainly and as readily recognisable as possible; whereas according to the artificial and unreal interpretation of Dr. Schulte a person would have to wade through an interminable field of endless controversies and contradictory assertions in order to attain, by the road along which Dr. Schulte conducts him, to the knowledge of what doctrine has been defined by the Church *de fide et moribus*. Why, Dr. Schulte enumerates above a hundred propositions, all the hundred, he says, 'dogmatic utterances,' out of those Bulls alone which he quotes. Surely this fact of itself ought to have shown him, nay, must have shown him, and made him say to himself, 'The Pope and the bishops never could by any possibility have meant or willed such an absurdity.'

Again, the Papal laws do not always rest their *motivum* or principle on divine teaching alone, but not unfrequently on a human view of the *Jus publicum*, as it was regarded in the period in which they were passed, or after thorough consideration of the measures which, according to human wisdom, were the best that could be adopted. We can easily see what a wild-goose chase we should be led if, every one for himself, we had to hunt up the supposed motives for ever so many Papal laws, in order to make out of them so many Papal infallible and unalterable definitions of faith!

(4.) In close connection with the foregoing is Dr. Schulte's further assertion that 'no one of the constitutions brought forward by him has in view *mere* ecclesiastical discipline, because he designedly omits all such mere matters of discipline.'

Perhaps Dr. Schulte really believes this is the case. But his assertion, that there is no one of these constitutions which has in view mere ecclesiastical discipline, is a statement utterly without foundation. If, according to the plain statement of the definition of the Vatican Council, we are bound to hold that infallible definitions of faith are unalterable, and if, on the other side, we have before our eyes the fact that Dr. Schulte's Papal constitutions are, with one exception, alterable, and, indeed, have in time past, been either altogether revoked, or have had important modifications made in them by other Papal constitutions, then it is as clear as day, that his assertion is utterly without foundation. Are we to suppose that the Bull for the organisation of the College of Cardinals belongs not to a mere disciplinary law of the Church, but really constitutes a dogma of faith or morals?

It may serve as a further proof how utterly void of foundation this assertion is, that among these constitutions there are several, which pronounce excommunication upon different persons.

Now the Council of Trent expressly says* that excommunication is 'the nerve of the Church's discipline.' Then, if this be so, bulls of excommunication must belong to the discipline of the Church.

(5.) Hereupon Dr. Schulte tries to prove that in the Church's laws we find the particular formulas adopted which the definition of the Vatican Council required for an infallible definition. He brings all sorts of reasons for this, none of them good reasons, and many of them have been already disposed of. Still there are some which require a more careful treatment.

When he says, that the formulation requisite for a definition of faith really exists whenever the constitutions of the Pope are directed 'generally to the whole Church,' or 'when they are sent out by virtue of his supreme apostolical power,' I maintain it in no way follows from this that these constitutions, by reason of these expressions, are definitions of faith. The Pope has the supreme authority in the Church even in other respects besides matters of faith and morals; if accordingly he makes use of the supreme authority which he possesses over other provinces of that power which he holds in the Church, even towards the whole Church,—still, this is not such a case as the definition of the Vatican Council had in view; no, not even if the constitution is directed to the whole Church, and is issued by virtue of the supreme apostolical power.

When Dr. Schulte lays such special weight upon

---

* *Canones et Decreta Concil. Trident.*, sessio 25, c. iii. De Reformat. Compare the Decretals of Pope Gregory IX., cap. v. De Consuetudinibus (i. 4).

the introduction to these constitutions, because, as he says, 'It is from these that we may gather the doctrine of the Popes,' I must positively declare that Popes never do smuggle their definitions of doctrine in this underhand way into the introduction of this or that Bull (a Bull, too, which perhaps does not treat of faith or morals), in such a manner that such a supposed definition may run the risk of remaining for centuries unnoticed and unacknowledged.*

Finally, when Dr. Schulte denies that the word *definire*, 'to define'—which is of such special weight in the Vatican Council—is not a technical expression having a special reference to definitions of faith, and strictly confined to them, I must most decidedly deny that assertion. When he says the Council of Trent has not made use of this word to designate its 'definitions of faith,' I answer: 'Is the Council of Trent the only general council? Are there not other councils? Let him examine them. He will then be able to convince himself that these ancient councils did commonly designate a definition of faith as *definitio fidei* or *definitio*, and used the word *definire* without any other addition. So did the General Council of Chalcedon; so did the Third Council of Con-

* Dr. Schulte really attributes to the Popes this absurd conduct, saying: 'It is to be regretted that people have not attended to the introductions to Bulls, principally, I suppose, on account of their lengthiness. This is a great mistake; as they are often the quintessence of the Bull. And yet this introduction itself shows that canonists up to this have not known the proper meaning of the Cardinals. Even Phillipps,' &c. (p. 36 of his Pamphlet). The Bull of which Dr. Schulte is here speaking is now nearly 300 years old, and it has been the good fortune of Dr. Schulte to discover a most important definition in its introduction, which up to this time has escaped the notice of all canonists. And this precious discovery is a definition *de fide !*

stantinople; so did the Second Council of Nicæa.* To say nothing of other councils, it ought to be enough to settle the matter to mention only the celebrated *definitio* of the Council of Florence, in which the *de fide* proposition on the primacy of the Roman Pontiff and his supreme teaching power in the Church was defined with the consent of the Greeks.† Perhaps Dr. Schulte may find reason to soften his own crabbed assertion: '*Definire* is not a technical word in the Church's language in deciding a doctrine; to make capital out of it, is as false in fact as it is absurd in theory,' if he will but peruse the acts of the councils I have mentioned, to say nothing of the use of the word in the science of theology and in the celebrated Papal definition *de fide* in our own times.‡

* *Concil. Chalcedon.* act. v. and vi. in Harduin's *Acta Concil.*, t. ii. col. 451, 455, 466 ; *Concil. Constpl. III.*, *Act* xviii. (Harduin, l. c. t. iii. col. 1394, 1395, 1399, 1455); *Concil. Nicæn. II.*, *Act* vii. and viii. (Harduin, l. c. t. iv. col. 451, 455, 483, 486).

† See *Definitio S. Œcumenicæ Synodi Florentinæ*, in Harduin, l. c. t. ix. col. 419 ; and in the same Council *Definimus S. Apostolicam Sedem et Romanum Pontificem*, &c. (ibid. col. 423), we may read the same words in cap. iii. of the *Constitutio Dogmatica Concilii Vaticani* of July 18, 1870.

‡ See the Dogmatic Bull of Pius IX., *Ineffabilis Deus* of Dec. 8, 1854. In which is defined the Immaculate Conception of the most holy Virgin Mary, with the words : 'Auctoritate declaramus, pronunciamus et DEFINIMUS doctrinam,' &c.

NOTE. The editor of the French translation here says, much to the purpose : 'In writing the above lines Mgr. Fessler, whose theological and historical erudition is so complete and so trustworthy, has failed to recall to mind several passages even more decisive against M. Schulte than those which he has quoted. M. Schulte asserts that this word "definire" has not been employed *even once* by the Council of Trent as a technical expression applicable to fix once for all a dogma. Instead of not being employed at all, it is, to our certain knowledge, employed at least six times ; session 13 and 21, at the end of the prooemium, "definitum ;" session 14 in the prooemium,

(6.) Again, Dr. Schulte asserts that 'any one may see for certain from the addition of the anathema whether a constitution of a Pope is a law or a doctrine, or both combined.' This, however, is quite untenable, because the 'anathema,' or, in other words, the penalty of excommunication, is pronounced for two reasons, either for deliberate unbelief in the face of a solemnly expressed and defined doctrine on faith or morals, or for disobedience to the Church's injunctions on some other matter. If the sincere recognition of a dogmatic proposition is demanded under the threat of an 'anathema,' then it is to be regarded as a sign of a definition. But if the threat of excommunication is annexed to a mere disciplinary law issued by the Pope, then submission, true obedience, is required in virtue of that power of jurisdiction which the Pope possesses in the Church.*

" definitionem ;" session 25 and last, at the end, twice " definita." Here is one of these passages : ' Sacrosancta Synodus . . . omnibus Christi fidelibus interdicit, ne postea de sanctissimæ eucharistiæ sacramento aliter credere, docere et prædicare audeant, quam ut est hoc præsenti decreto declaratum et *definitum*' (Sess. 13 prooem.). In another passage, session 14, prooem, the Council sets forth how important it is to give the sacrament of Penance ' pleniorem *definitionem*.' In the decree *De Recipiendis et Observandis Decretis Concilii*, at the end of the twenty-fifth and last session, the Council declares that it has had a special case, ' ut præcipuos hæreticorum nostri temporis errores damnaret et anathematizaret ; veramque et Catholicam doctrinam traderet et doceret, prout damnavit anathematizavit et *definivit*.' It cannot then be said that in these passages of the Council of Trent the word ' definire' is not used as a technical expression to fix a dogma once for all. TRANSLATOR.

* In another place Dr. Schulte makes another assertion, resting, as he says, upon Papal *ex cathedrâ* declarations, ' Acts purely of jurisdiction have a dogmatic character' (p. 55 of his work). This he endeavours to prove from the excommunication attached. But, I ask, what does he mean by the expression ' have a dogmatic cha-

This I will make plain by an example with which Dr. Schulte himself provides us. Alexander VI. drew a line in the ocean from the North Pole, and assigned to King Ferdinand and Queen Isabella of Spain all the continent and all the islands to the west of this imaginary line. He did this under the threat of excommunication against all those who should endeavour to encroach upon those countries without their permission.* Well, it is here quite clear that, in order not to fall under this excommunication, it was enough to keep your distance from the lands which the Pope had thus assigned; this most assuredly was no definition of faith.

(7.) I cannot conclude these remarks upon the particular assertions in this portion of Dr. Schulte's work without a general remark on the extraordinary way in which, in this Pamphlet, he assails the definition of the Vatican Council on the Infallible teaching office of the Roman Pontiff. He gives out that he is attacking one thing; but all the while he is really attacking something else. He professes to be assailing the definition of the Vatican Council; but in reality he is only assailing a theological opinion of the schools, which was in existence long before the Vatican Council, and which is neither confirmed nor rejected by the definition of the Council, but remains just what it was before. However, even

---

racter"? This is one of those vague expressions neither theological nor canonistic, the meaning of which has to be determined before it can be intelligible. It does not occur in any one of the passages which he quotes in proof of his assertion; and Dr. Schulte's conversion of the condemned propositions into positive *de fide* definitions and Papal utterances has thus had the unfortunate result of preventing him from ever seeing their real meaning.

* *Bullar. Rom.* ed. cit. t. iii. p. iii. pp. 234-235.

amongst those theologians who defended the thesis that the Infallibility of the Church extended even to general laws of the Church upon matters of discipline, *decreta disciplinæ*, there never was any one who, as Dr. Schulte supposes, went so far as to assert that every expression in the laws issued by the Pope, even when merely introductory, a declaration of the intention of punishing, the words of the judgments, the penal sentences passed, nay, even the motives leading to the issuing of such laws, must *all* be looked upon as infallible utterances of the Pope *ex cathedrâ*. Dr. Schulte stands alone in this extravagant assertion. The Vatican Council never taught this, nor did the science of theology ever teach it. Dr. Schulte assails what never existed, save in his own imagination.

34. And now I come to the last of what he calls 'our evasions.' He feels himself obliged to call it a mere evasion to say that no conclusion can be drawn from the particular acts or dealings of Popes as to what is and is not the doctrine of the Church. Supposing Popes have even deposed sovereigns, given away nations and countries, dissolved subjects from their solemn oaths of allegiance, &c., it does not follow that these transactions were doctrines of the Church, or that they rest upon an unalterable infallible definition. 'This, too,' he adds, 'was what in former times I have always myself asserted, believed, and taught; as I can prove any moment by several quotations from my earlier works, and the expressions I made use of, as the occasion presented itself, in reviews. But since the 18th of July 1870, there has remained for me and for everybody the alternative: This definition of chapter iv. (and iii.) of the Vatican Council, the so-called *Constitutio dogmatica de Ecclesia*,

is not to be recognised as the conclusion of a truly Ecumenical Council; or I must also acknowledge as unalterable doctrine of the Church those principles which the Popes have either directly enunciated, or which present themselves to us with logical cogency as the irresistible presumptions created by their proceedings in the government of the Church' (p. 62 of Dr. Schulte's work).

There is more than one thing to answer here. First and foremost I will give Dr. Schulte the consoling assurance that whatever he says he formerly asserted, believed, and taught about the deposition of sovereigns, he may now, after the Vatican definition, as far as that is concerned, go on asserting, believing, and teaching.* In saying this perhaps I

* On July 20, 1871, after the publication of Bishop Fessler's pamphlet, Pope Pius IX. received a deputation of the Academy of the Catholic religion. He exhorted its members to do their best to refute with all possible care the statements of those who made it their business to misconstrue the meaning of the Infallibility of the Pope, declaring it to be a pernicious error, to represent the Infallibility as comprising in itself the right to dethrone sovereigns, and release their subjects from their oath of allegiance. 'This right,' the Pope said, 'has, indeed, been exercised by Popes in extreme cases, but the right has absolutely nothing in common with Papal Infallibility. It was a result of the *Jus publicum* then in force by the consent of Christian nations, who recognised in the Pope the supreme judge of Christendom, and constituted him judge over princes and peoples even in temporal matters. The present situation is quite different. Nothing but bad faith could confound things so different and ages so dissimilar; as if an infallible judgment delivered upon some revealed truth had any analogy with a prerogative which the Popes, solicited by the desire of the people, have had to exercise when the public weal demanded it! Such statements are nothing but a mere pretext to excite princes against the Church.' The Pope's approbation of the Pastoral Instruction of the Swiss Bishops, in which this declaration of his is referred to, renders its authenticity indubitable. FRENCH TRANSLATOR.

expose myself to the danger of being classed with those good people whom he designates as 'mere children,' 'the ignorant multitude,' &c., p. 63; but for all that I must run this risk, and am unable, in spite of my danger, to refrain from stating this conviction. But then I must go on to say that I most emphatically decline the alternative he has offered me in such decisive language. I decline it as altogether unsound; and I confidently assert the Vatican Council *is* undoubtedly a truly Ecumenical Council, and its definition *is* to be accepted and acknowledged by every Catholic as the definition of an Ecumenical Council; and yet that it by no means follows (as Dr. Schulte says) that we are obliged to acknowledge ' as unalterable Catholic doctrine those principles which the Popes have either directly enunciated, or which present themselves to us with logical cogency as the irresistible presumptions created by their proceedings in the government of the Church;' but that the only thing which does follow from receiving the Vatican definition is,—that everybody must accept as a doctrine of the Church's faith and morals whatsoever the Pope in the exercise of his supreme teaching office declares and defines (*definit*) to be held by the Universal Church as doctrine of faith and morals.*

* Accordingly not all, by a great deal, that the Pope has, it may be, even directly expressed, as Dr. Schulte says, still less what can be gathered indirectly from acts of ecclesiastical government, can be considered as affording 'an irresistible presumption.' The Popes often express or infer principles which are acknowledged in the *Jus publicum* of the age in which they lived, when those principles were by no means doctrines *de fide et moribus*. In Ballerini (*De vi et ratione Roman Pontificis*, c. xv. § x. n. 38 and 41) we may find an exposition of this as complete as it is instructive.

K

If, however, Dr. Schulte is determined to stand by his assertion, that from the irresistible presumptions created by acts in the government of the Church, principles must be inferred which must themselves be regarded as the doctrine of the Church, then I would call his attention to the fact that General Councils too have deposed sovereigns and released subjects from their allegiance; as for instance the first General Council of Lyons, in the year 1245.* Thus the point of his proof is directed not against Popes, but against the Universal Church. Among other reasons for his assertion that it is a mere evasion to say the Vatican definition of the Infallible teaching office of the Roman Pontiff has no reference to his proceedings in the government of the Church, but only to his definitions of doctrine, Dr. Schulte, besides repetitions of what he has already said, mentions one which I cannot pass over in silence. He says, 'The "clausula" form into which the Infallibility is thown is a thoroughly arbitrary proceeding;' and he adds in confirmation of this sentiment, 'Where has Christ bound up His words in clauses and formulas?' This is plainly to give the Church a downright slap in the face, and to condemn all General Councils from Nicæa to Trent. For they have one and all, as often as they made a definition on faith or morals, expressed it in the most definite terms (what Dr. Schulte calls 'clauses' and 'formulas'), in order to obviate, as far as possible, all error, doubt, and misunderstanding. It was precisely because the Vatican Council wished to prevent, as well as it could, erroneous interpretations of its definition, that it declared in the simplest and most easily intelligible words, in what kind of operations,

* Harduin, *Acta Concil.* t. vii. col. 385, 386.

and under what conditions, the Pope was to be looked upon as Infallible. It is sheer perversity to assail a definition of the Church which precisely defines and limits its subject matter, in order to remove all occasion of giving unfounded anxieties, misapprehensions, and misapplications, which might tend to disturb the conscience, simply because of *its very definiteness;* to reject its putting its definitions into clauses, and to talk of its being arbitrary ; and then afterwards, rejecting its own prescribed limitations and doing violence to its plain language and its true signification, to extend the definition perversely in a most unwarrantable manner to provinces with which it has nothing whatever to do; and all this to the great disturbance of men's minds, and to the injury of the Church.

CHAPTER V.

'CONSIDERATIONS ON THE STATE LAW.'

35. UNDER this title Dr. Schulte collects together as proven (Ger. *bewiesen*), to use his own word, all that he has gathered together out of different rescripts and proceedings of Popes, and in his own thirteen propositions, to be infallible and unalterable Catholic doctrine, which every one is bound to accept, if he accepts as a *de fide* proposition the definition of the Vatican Council on the Infallible teaching office of the Roman Pontiff.

I have proved, in sections 15-27 of my answer to him on each of his thirteen propositions, that, upon the principle laid down in the definition of the Vatican Council 'on the Infallible teaching office of the Roman Pontiff, they are *not* to be regarded as Catholic doctrine *de fide*, that they are *not* Papal utterances *ex cathedrâ*, and accordingly are *not* unalterable.

I had shown previously (section 13), that the other assertion which he brought in connection with his thirteen propositions, that he had no warrant whatever for saying that 'it had been declared *ex cathedrâ* that Popes have *never* overstepped the limits of their powers; that they have *never* erred in their canons and constitutions; that their constitutions rest, as it were, upon Divine inspiration;' for in reality no Pope *ever* has declared this *ex cathedrâ*, nor set it forth as a definition *de fide.* Having proved this, the edifice of consequences, built by Dr. Schulte upon his worthless foundation, falls to the ground.

Still I must select one proposition, introduced by him as a corollary, which should not remain unnoticed. He says, ' The limitation of the omnipotence of the Popes upon earth rests merely with their own will.' This is a proposition which may well shock anybody. But happily, first and foremost, it is altogether wrong to speak of a Pope's omnipotence.. The Pope has from Christ, in the person of St. Peter, received the fulness of power,* which means, as the Ecumenical Council of Florence accurately explained, the full power to feed the whole Church, to lead and to rule it. If people choose to call this Papal omnipotence, then they will be really ousting an expression which has its own perfect justification, and its right meaning in the language of the Church, and foisting into its place a newly-coined expression, ' Papal omnipotence.' This is a term which the language of the Church has never used of Popes, which gives a wholly erroneous impression, and which in unlearned people would be apt to awaken the most strange apprehensions. Much more will this be the case when, as Dr. Schulte adds, this Papal omnipotence is supposed to have no restriction but the will of the Pope. All this is a monstrous untruth. The Papal power, not Papal omnipotence, has its restrictions in the laws of God, and in the will of God, not in the will of the Pope.†

* Plenitudo potestatis.

† I would here direct Dr. Schulte's attention to Walter's excellent exposition in his *Ecclesiastical Law*, sec. 126 (thirteenth edition), on ' The Pope's power not arbitrary and unlimited.' With this, however, a canonist ought to be already acquainted; and perhaps

All, then, which Dr. Schulte asserts on this ground, all that he asserts of the power of the Pope against heretics, and of the obligation of Catholics to obey the Pope, and also of the binding power of excommunication, is, so far as the Vatican definition is concerned, left just where it was before.

When, then, he draws his conclusion from such unwarrantable assumptions that no non-Catholic sovereign in his position as ruler is secure of his throne; no government carried on by those who are not Catholics is secure of its authority; no non-Catholic is secure of his life, or his freedom, or his honour, or his property; and what is more, under certain circumstances, no Catholic ruler, no government carried on even by Catholics, no individual Catholic, is a whit more secure,—then I must be pardoned for saying that all these assertions are as utterly ludicrous as they are untrue (see no. 28-9). Had not he better have said outright, 'Nobody is now safe from the Pope'? Any true Catholic, who, according to the true old Catholic doctrine, knows that the Pope is the pastor appointed by God over all the faithful, that he is their father and their teacher, will never believe a man is *now* a whit the less safe from the Pope.

Less safe, forsooth! Why? Because an express assurance has now been given him that the Pope, as teacher of all Christians, cannot err or lead others into error in definitions which he makes for all the Church upon faith or morals!

It is indeed very probable that those who are not

Dr. Schulte will answer, 'That is all valueless now since the Infallibility declaration.' But what is there said is just as true *now* as it was before.

Catholics, and who on that account are, through want of knowledge, the easier led astray and bewildered, will be disturbed by such a spectre as Dr. Schulte has evoked, when told that this is the result of modern Catholic teaching. In behalf of all such persons I make this express declaration: that all rulers and governments and subjects, Catholic and non-Catholic, are, since the Vatican definition of Infallibility, just as safe in their persons, in their life, in their freedom, honour, and possessions as they were before. Dr. Schulte says the contrary; but the facts which he alleges do not belong to the province of Infallibility, and so they make nothing for his assertion. 'Crying "wolf!" is a poor joke,' is an old proverb which might here be very properly applied.

In conclusion, Dr. Schulte directs the State to be sure to take stringent measures to protect itself from the Pope. Such measures will either be pointed against the Pope or else against us Catholics. I should be surprised indeed if any statesman should resolve, as Dr. Schulte suggests, to require the Pope to make some contradictory declaration in respect of his Infallibility; if he were to do so, he would have nobody to blame but himself for this exhibition of folly, and few people like to make fools of themselves. And I should also doubt if any statesman would venture to require Catholics to take an oath, or make a solemn declaration, in respect of the Infallibility of the Pope, since experienced politicians know well how dangerous it is to meddle with freedom of faith and conscience, especially in countries where full freedom of faith and conscience is secured to all alike.

Wise statesmen do not forget the lessons given by the facts of the present time. Let any man look at the events which have happened in Europe since July 18th, 1870, down to December last, and ask himself what steps the Popes of the Middle Ages, whose spectres Dr. Schulte has conjured up from their graves to terrify the children of modern times, would have taken in the face of such events in all countries, especially in France? And what has Pius IX. done? He has but used gentle, fatherly, tender-hearted words full of Christian love and humanity towards France* and towards King William of Prussia.

36. A real statesman, looking with deeper glance into the great questions of the present and of the past, whose emblem is not the staff of the policeman surmounting the fasces of authority, will entertain very different thoughts. He will, if I mistake not, be disposed to think that it well becomes a religion revealed by God, a Church founded by God, to have an organ by means of which, according to the will of God, and through God's special assistance, the Divine doctrine may ever be preserved unfalsified, without admixture of any human error.

---

* The Archbishop of Tours, whom the Pope intrusted with the mission to intervene with France in behalf of peace, wrote an excellent letter on the subject to the French Government. 'The powers of Europe,' he said, 'in times long past, times which formed Christendom to be what it afterwards became, were wont to appeal to the Pope in their contests with each other to act as their umpire; and many a time the intervention of the Pope has brought peace and welfare to their people. The Holy Father does not now complain that people have ceased to take him to be their arbitrator. He does but assume for himself the liberty to sigh over our miseries, and the right to entreat for the life of his children. Happy am I indeed if my mission to you, a mission which I esteem the honour of my life, were destined to give effect to the hopes of the Head of the Church, which are so fully in accord with the feelings of the whole of Europe.'

He will consider that since from its origin for all time the Infallibility of the Catholic Church in respect of faith and morals is secured, it is merely a question for the Church to judge of for herself, whether, according to the tradition of the Christian faith, preserved from the beginning, the Pope *and* the Bishops, or whether the Pope *without* the Bishops, possessed this gift of Infallibility.

He will consider that oppression of the conscience of the Catholic population in matters of faith through the imposition of an oath or a solemn declaration will be always and everywhere regarded as a kind of persecution, as was the case in England and Ireland, where this practice was for some time adopted, but where it has been now discontinued.

He will consider that it ill becomes a true liberal-minded statesman to establish such a persecution, especially when measures of that sort are adopted merely in the distant prospect of a barely possible danger.

He will consider that the steps the Pope has actually taken, and his whole conduct in the last half year (1870) that has passed since the definition was pronounced, have not only given no real ground for alarm to Governments or to our brethren who are separated from the Catholic Church, but on the contrary have guaranteed as far as was possible their most perfect tranquillity.

I conclude with the earnest desire that what I have here written in the cause of Truth may in all it contains serve that same Truth, and that in all who may read it it may advance the knowledge of the Truth.

INDEX.

ACTS OF POPES. Simple acts of Popes, no. 14 (2), p. 64; acts of their ecclesiastical government, no. 14 (4), p. 65; as for instance Concordats, p. 77; what is the bearing of Papal Infallibility upon all such acts? no. 18, end, p. 82; whether the principles supposed to be implied in the ecclesiastical government of the Popes are infallible definitions? p. 20; acts of Popes brought forward by Dr. Schulte, and examined by Bp. Fessler—depositions of sovereigns, donations of countries, penal sentences, &c., no. 17 (2), pp. 70, 71, 72; what we ought to think of such acts considered in themselves? note, p. 71.

ANATHEMA. Whether the fact of a Papal constitution being accompanied by an anathema, or, in other words, by a sentence of excommunication, shows decisively, or not, that the constitution is a dogmatic definition? no. 33 (6), end, p. 125, cf. p. 119.

APOSTOLICAL AUTHORITY. Are all Papal constitutions which have been made in virtue of their supreme apostolical authority definitions *ex cathedrâ*? p. 82, cf. p. 122.

AUTHORS QUOTED BY BISHOP FESSLER.
Ballerini, p. 43, pp. 46, 55, notes.
Bellarmine, p. 48 text, and p. 55, note.
Benedict XIV., as private Doctor, pp. 114, 115, 118, notes.
Canus, Melchior, p. 46, note.
Guibert, Mgr., p. 136, note.
Hurter, Frederick, pp. 106, 107.
Melchers, Mgr., p. 21.
Perrone, p. 43, note.
Savigny, De, p. 104, note.
 By French Translator :
Swiss Bishops, pp. 62, 63, notes.
Trent, Council of, pp. 124, 125, note.

BISHOPS. Whether the Bull of Sixtus V. and the third Chapter of the Vatican Council have taken from the Bishops any part of their former rights and dignities? p. 80.

140   *Index.*

BRIEFS OF POPES. *Multiplices inter* of Pius IX., is it *ex cathedrâ ?* p. 58, and preface, p. 11, cf. p. 61, note.

BULLS. Are we to look for dogmatic definitions in the introduction to Papal Bulls? p. 123 and note ; a Bull addressed to the whole Church, and signed by all the Cardinals, is it an infallible dogmatic definition ? p. 74, cf. p. 122.

BULLS quoted by Bishop Fessler :

Quia Fridericus	1239, Gregory IX., p. 71.
Cum adversus	1243, Innocent IV., p. 95.
Ad Apostolicæ	1245, same Pope, p. 72.
Ad extirpanda	1252, same Pope, p. 95.
Unam sanctam	1302, Boniface VIII., p. 67 and following.
Romanus Pontifex	1454, Nicholas V., p. 81.
Inter sollicitudines	1515, Leo X., p. 85.
Divina disponente	1516, same Pope, p. 77.
Pastor æternus	1516, same Pope, p. 86.
Exsurge Domine	1520, same Pope, p. 56, cf. pp. 53, 92.
Ejus qui	1535, Paul III., p. 72.
Cum Redemptor	1538, same Pope, p. 72.
Cum quorundam	1555, Paul IV., p. 96.
Cum ex Apostolatus	1559, same Pope, p. 73, and Preface, pp. 8, 9.
Regnans in excelsis	1570, Pius V., p. 72.
Postquam verus	1586, Sixtus V., p. 80.
Zelo domus Dei	1648, Innocent X., p. 89.
Auctorem fidei	1794, Pius VI., p. 92.
Apostolicæ Sedis moderationi	1869, Pius IX., pp. 88, 89.
In cœna Domini	„ pp. 94, 126.

CHURCH (UNIVERSAL). Whether it follows that a constitution is *ex cathedrâ* from being addressed to the universal Church ? p. 122, and p. 74, note.

COUNCIL OF THE VATICAN. Examination of different facts relative to the Council of the Vatican, pp. 15, 16 ; text of the chapter on the infallible teaching office of the Roman Pontiff, p. 33 ; explanations of this chapter, p. 41.

CONDEMNATION OF BOOKS. Is a Papal decree condemning a bad book an infallible decision ? p. 58.

DEFINIRE. Reflections on this word as a technical theological expression, pp. 119, 124, and note.

DEFINITIONS OF THE FAITH. Whether definitions of the faith require to be published in any special form, in order to bind the conscience ? p. 22.

DEFINITION EX CATHEDRA. Explanation of this term, p. 9 (1); by what notes a definition *ex cathedrâ* can be known, p. 52, cf. p. 70

Index. 141

no. 16, end ; whether it follows from a Papal constitution being addressed to the universal Church, or promulgated by virtue of the Pope's supreme apostolical authority, that it must, on that account, be regarded as a definition *ex cathedrâ?* p. 122, cf. 74, note ; to what matters an *ex cathedrâ* definition extends? p. 53 ; whether all that is found in a dogmatic Decree or Bull—as, for instance, the introductions and preambles—are to be regarded as definitions *ex cathedrâ?* p. 46 ; are there a great or a small number of definitions *ex cathedrâ?* p. 53. See also the heads INSPIRATION and INFALLIBILITY.

DEPOSITION OF PRINCES. Whether the right which Popes have exercised in the Middle Ages of deposing princes has anything in common with Papal Infallibility? p. 128 and note ; whether Œcumenical Councils have ever exercised the right of deposing princes? p. 130.

DISCIPLINE. Whether ecclesiastical discipline belongs to the domains of Infallibility? pp. 45, 65, 118 ; whether disciplinary laws are unalterable? pp. 118-119.

GOSPEL. Whether definitions *ex cathedrâ* can be likened to the HOLY GOSPEL? p 80.

GOVERNMENT OF THE CHURCH. See ACTS OF POPES.

HERETICS. What conclusion is to be drawn as to a Papal declaration whereby a doctrine has been declared heretical? p. 70 ; in what sense it is possible to admit in theory that a Pope may be heretical? p. 75 ; the different position the Church has assumed externally towards heretics at different epochs of her existence, pp. 107, 108, 109; whether the penal laws against heretics are to be considered as doctrinal definitions, and unalterable ? p. 96.

INFALLIBILITY. Why this general expression 'Infallibility' was avoided by the Vatican Council? p. 38 ; explanation of the true meaning of the constitution of the Vatican Council on the infallible teaching office of the Roman Pontiff, pp. 39-47 ; whether the Pope possesses the gift of Infallibility in the exercise of all his official prerogatives? p. 42 ; in what cases he does possess this privilege, p. 43, cf. notes at end of chapter ii. See also the word DEFINITION *ex cathedrâ.*

INSPIRATION. Whether the Pope, when he pronounces a definition *ex cathedrâ,* is directly inspired by God, as the Prophets were of old, or whether he is assisted by a special grace attached to his office, which prevents him from going wrong when he is formulating the faith of the Church, contained in Scripture and tradition? pp. 81, 46, and see notes A and B, end of c. ii.

INTENTION. Whether the intention of the Pope to make such and such a declaration dogmatic—an intention not expressed, but re-

142   Index.

sulting from certain facts—can cause it to be regarded as a dogmatic definition ? p. 69.

JUS PENALE. Whether the Popes are infallible in the domain of penal law, even in ecclesiastical penal law? p. 73, cf. p. 45.

JUS PUBLICUM. Whether the principles recognised in the Jus Publicum of the Middle Ages exercised an influence upon the acts and declarations of Popes at those times ? p. 120, cf. p. 103-105.

LEGISLATION (ECCLESIASTICAL). Whether the Papal laws have always had divine doctrine for their foundation and origin? p. 120; whether the principles on which the ecclesiastical legislation of the Popes was founded, and from which it started, ought to be counted as infallible definitions? pp. 120-121.

OMNIPOTENCE. Whether the expression, 'Omnipotence of the Pope,' is admissible? p. 133, cf. p. 53.

POPE. Whether the Pope, in the province ecclesiastical, always acts as Pope, as Head of the Church ? p. 114, note.

PENAL LAWS and SENTENCES. Whether penal enactments of Popes, penal sentences pronounced by them, have anything to do with Infallibility? pp. 86, 96-98.

PERSONA PRIVATA of the Pope. Distinction between the Pope considered as Pope and considered as a private person. Whether the Pope can err in matters of faith as a private person ? pp. 113-115, cf. 76 ; supposing the Pope to write books as an author, whether it is necessary to hold the ideas on religious matters to which he there gives expression' to be definitions *ex cathedrâ?* p. 115, cf. p. 65.

PLAN of Mgr. Fessler's work, pp. 13-14.

PROPOSITIONS (DOCTRINAL). Whether the doctrinal propositions attributed to the Popes by Dr. Schulte ought to be regarded as infallible definitions? p. 101 ; examination of the declarations and acts of the Popes from which Dr. Schulte has drawn these doctrinal propositions, p. 64-102; what ought we to think of these declarations and acts in themselves? p. 71, and note, pp. 103-110.

POWER OF THE POPE. What '*objecta*' — *i.e.* subject-matter — come under the power of the Popes? pp. 42-44 ; with regard to what portion or portions of this subject-matter has Infallibility been conferred upon the Pope? p. 44 ; what is the duty of a Catholic in all these matters, even in those matters to which Infallibility is not applicable? p. 44, cf. p. 61, note.

SYLLABUS. Is the Syllabus one of those doctrinal propositions of which the Vatican Council speaks ? pp. 92-93, and preface, p. 11 ; examination of a passage of the Syllabus, p. 94, cf. pp. 59-61.

TEACHING OFFICE. Is it true, as Dr. Schulte says, that Holy Scripture does not contain any passage relative to the teaching office of St. Peter? p. 116; why, among the different functions of the supreme ecclesiastical power, 'the teaching office' alone has received from God a special grace? p. 117. Infallibility of the Papal teaching office, see INFALLIBILITY.

THEOLOGY. What is the special business of theology as regards revealed truth? p. 17.

UNALTERABLE. What the Vatican Council means by saying that the decisions *ex cathedrâ* are by their nature unalterable? p. 46; are the disciplinary laws of the Popes unalterable? p. 47.

www.ingramcontent.com/pod-product-compliance
Lightning Source LLC
Chambersburg PA
CBHW030313170426
43202CB00009B/991